MACRAMÉ FOR BEGINNERS

SPARK YOUR CREATIVITY AND TRANSFORM YOUR HOME DECOR WITH EXCEPTIONAL DIY MACRAMÉ PROJECTS WITH THE COMPREHENSIVELY EXPLAINED STEP-BY-STEP AND EASY-TO-FOLLOW PROJECT IDEAS

[Justine Lindsey]

© Copyright 2021 - All rights reserved.

The content contained within this book may not be reproduced, duplicated or transmitted without direct written permission from the author or the publisher.

Under no circumstances will any blame or legal responsibility be held against the publisher, or author, for any damages, reparation, or monetary loss due to the information contained within this book. Either directly or indirectly.

Legal Notice:

This book is copyright protected. This book is only for personal use. You cannot amend, distribute, sell, use, quote or paraphrase any part, or the content within this book, without the consent of the author or publisher.

Disclaimer Notice:

Please note the information contained within this document is for educational and entertainment purposes only. All effort has been executed to present accurate, up to date, and reliable, complete information. No warranties of any kind are declared or implied. Readers acknowledge that the author is not engaging in the rendering of legal, financial, medical or professional advice. The content within this book has been derived from various sources. Please consult a licensed professional before attempting any techniques outlined in this book.

By reading this document, the reader agrees that under no circumstances is the author responsible for any losses, direct or indirect, which are incurred as a result of the use of information contained within this document, including, but not limited to, — errors, omissions, or inaccuracies.

Table of Contents

INTRODUCTION 7
CHAPTER 1: HISTORY OF MACRAMÉ 10
CHAPTER 2: BENEFITS OF MACRAMÉ 18
CHAPTER 3: MACRAMÉ TOOLBOX 30
Macramé Materials 30
Cord Measurement 32
Finishing Techniques 36
Difference Between A String SA Rope And A Cord 41
Tools Required For Macramé 43
Beginner Guide To Macrame Cord And Metal Shapes 48
CHAPTER 4: HOW TO GET STARTED TO MACRAME – THE BASIC KNOTS 53
Lark's Head Knot 54
Turn around Lark's Head Knot 57
Capuchin Knot 60
Crown Knot 63
Askew Double Half-tie 67
Frivolite Knot 70
Flat Double Half-hitch 74
Josephine Knot 76
CHAPTER 5: MACRAME IMPORTANT TIPS AND TRICKS 78
Picking Materials And Prepping Yourworkspace, Cord Preparation, Finishing Techniques, Begin With Simple Knots 78
Attend A Workshop, Saveyour Left-Over Chord, Study Online 81
Have Fun, Macramé Supplies, Difference Between A String, Rope, And Rope Tools Required For Macramé 85
CHAPTER 6: TECHNIQUES AND SUGGESTIONS 89

Utilizing respectable quality rope 92
Keep it straightforward 92
Keep your strain even 93
Go to a Workshop 93
Save Your Left-Over Cord 94

CHAPTER 7: HOUSE AND GARDEN PROJECTS 95
Jar hanger 95
Wall hangings 101
Charming earrings 108
Hexnut bracelet 113

CHAPTER 8: BRACELET PROJECTS 118
Materials Required In The Project 118
Prodedure: 119

CHAPTER 9: MACRAMÉ NECKLACES 123
Yarn Twisted Necklace 123
Leathery Knotted Necklace 125
Silky Purple Necklace 128
Macramé Gem Necklace 131
Nautical Rope Necklace 134
Macramé Tie-Dye Necklace 136

CHAPTER 10: MACRAMÉ EARRINGS 139
Summery Chevron Earrings 139
Macramé Spiral Earrings 142
Fringe Fun Earrings 145
Day Glow Earrings 148
Hearty Paperclip Earrings 151

CHAPTER 11: OTHER MACRAMÉ JEWELRY 153
Sun and Moon Anklet 153
Macramé Rhinestone Ring 155
Easy Macramé Ring 158

Macramé Watch Strand 161

CHAPTER 12: TERMINOLOGIES USED 163

Alternating 163

Adjacent 164

Alternating Square Knots (ASK) 164

Bar 165

Bangle 165

Band 166

Buttonhole (BH) 166

Bundle 167

Braided Cord 167

Body 168

Bight 168

Crook 169

Cord 169

Combination Knot 170

Cloisonne 170

Chinese Crown Knot 171

Charm 171

Doubled 172

Double Half Hitch (DHH) 172

Diagonal 173

Distance across 173

Fusion Knots 174

Fringe 174

Flax Linen 175

Finishing Knot 175

Holding Cord 176

Hitch 176

Inverted 176

Interlace 177

MICRO-MACRAMÉ 177
METALLIC 177
MOUNT 178
NETTING 178
ORGANIZE 179
PICOT 179
PENDANT 180
SYNTHETIC 180
SYMMETRY 181
STANDING END 181
TEXTURE 182
TENSION OR TAUT 182
VERTICAL 183
WORKING END 183
WEAVE 184
TOOLS AND MATERIALS 184
YARN 184
METAL WIRE 185
NEEDLES 186
TAPE 186
GARMENTS RACK 186
CORD 187
OTHERS ARE: 187

CHAPTER 13: TIPS AND TRICKS ON HOW TO MAKE DIFFERENT KNOTS FOR BEGINNERS 190

CHAPTER 14: BASIC TECHNIQUES FOR KNITTING 194

CONCLUSION 201

Introduction

Macramé is excellence exemplified, and the one thing we as a whole love to do is make these wonders ourselves, which gives us incredible fulfillment. Verifying Macramé plans can be entrusting for novices and surprisingly a few experts. Being here doesn't mean you need to surrender; you simply need more data.

Anyway, would you say you are attempting to make diverse Macramé plans without any result? Have you effectively made diverse macramé plans, yet have this one plan that is to a greater extent a test for you? Or then again have you been having difficulties getting a book that gives you every one of the basics you need to begin and complete a macramé plan?

This book will assist you with settling the entirety of the difficulties you have identified with the production of your macramé plans. It utilizes the best concept, which is the utilization of visuals. You need to comprehend that learning macramé is about visuals instead of articulations that are difficult to follow.

We have unique bit by bit picture headings that can bring you from the start down to the end with no disarray at all. The data gave here won't just assist you with beginning and finish your macramé plans, yet additionally will assist you with seeing a portion of the mix-ups you may have been making en route.

Thus, investigating the plans and steps in this book gives you the functional edge to make the best plans even past your assumption. The one thing you can depend on with regards to DIY books is reasonableness, and the degree of common sense that accompanies this book is something you can depend trust.

Buying this book would be an extraordinary expansion to your assortment since you don't simply get data, which is incredible, yet you likewise get a vibe of what you are doing on the grounds that, with each progression, you see whether you are moving the correct way. Trust me, you will partake in the means since it will be just about as extraordinary as seeing a plane taking off through the skies.

Go along with me as we go through different macramé plans, become familiar with the advantages you will get from making them for yourself, just as some extra data you will require.

Chapter 1: History Of Macramé

From the hour of the Arabic weavers in the thirteenth century, macramé was an artistic expression that acquired prominence and continuously spread everywhere, spreading joy and a feeling of fulfillment among individuals of various societies. Macramé is a straightforward, old art of hitching in mathematical examples to make some profoundly inventive things. An assortment of things might be produced using adornments and home plan merchandise to plant holders and divider holders. It is a talented type of workmanship that figures out how to put different mathematical examples on articles without utilizing snares, snares or bands. The key hubs utilized in this work of art include square hubs and hitching shapes. This type of craftsmanship is not difficult to learn and was utilized and polished for mariners on long excursions together by the illustrious patios. A portion of the normal materials and crude materials utilized in macramée were cotton twiny, hemp, calfskin and yarn to give some delightful gems shape to different home embellishments. This part gives an intriguing and magnificent data on the beginning and foundation of the artistic expression, 'Macramé.'

Intriguing and mind boggling data about Macramé's starting point and foundation

It is said that Macramé arose in the thirteenth century, alongside the Arab weavers. These artificials hitched overabundance string and yarn along the edges of hand-lingered textures to make enlivening edges on shower towels, wraps and cloak. The craftsmanship got its name from the Arabic word 'Migramah' signifying 'striped towel,' 'elaborate periphery' or 'tacky cover.'

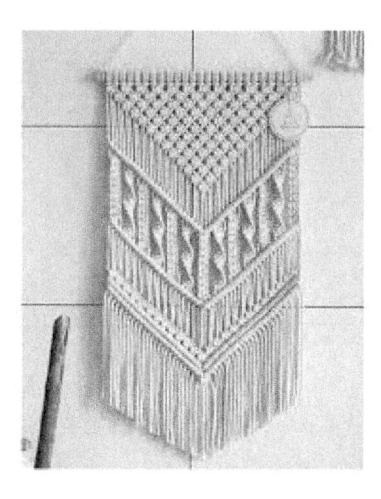

There are a few records from the set of experiences pages which express that Macramé was likewise acted in the fourteenth and fifteenth hundreds of years in France and Italy. France has a past filled with delivering huge amounts of Macramé and chronicled information projects that during those days it was viewed as a set up craftsmanship.

After the Moorish success, the craftsmanship was taken to Spain, and afterward spread all through Europe. All through the late seventeenth century it was first brought to England at the court of

Queen Mary II, who was so attached to the method that she began to consider the specialty all through Holland. During the 1780s, it is likewise said that Queen Charlotte, George III's better half, was occupied with tying Macramé edges to embellish her court. This was the initial move towards the craftsmanship 's prominence, after which Macramé started to acquaint himself with different pieces of the world. For some, societies, taking on the work of art was simple in light of the fact that their way of life offered something almost identical to the tying that was done in Macramé.

Macramé gems likewise became well known in the mid seventies among American neo-radical and grit swarm. The gems producers utilized square bunches and granny bunches to make the gems, alongside hand tailored glass dabs. They likewise utilized the regular components like bone and shell to give the trimmings a brightening finish. Macramé adornments highlighted belt, anklets and wristbands.

Macramé then, at that point turned out to be enormously famous among the nineteenth century British and North American mariners who spent extended periods of time cruising to tie bunches and hitch ties. They used to make haggle cover edges, and mesh and screens on their long excursions. These mariners then, at that point utilized the items and the articles made in the deal with China and India, consequently advocating the craftsmanship in the Asian piece of the world. Large numbers of the best Macramé models hitched by these mariners can be found at the Church Institute of the Seamen in New York City.

In the Victorian time frame, the fine art accomplished most prevalence with practically all families contemplating and having the specialty in their garments. Macramé Lace's book of Sylvia (1882) tells the perusers the best way to work with rich decorations for dark and bright dress, including for home wear, garden party wear, ocean side ramblings and balls.

Macrame form has focused on various reasonable curios in the mid twentieth century. These items included totes, belts, rope, cords, pulls and ringer pulls, light and shade. During a similar period, craftsmen kept on delivering wraps and totes as their local art in Portugal, Ecuador, and Mexico, in spite of the fact that Macramé currently focused on a progression of articles.

This extraordinary Macramé craftsmanship was no special case, similar to every one of the things that succeed or face their destruction. Out of disregard the abilities started to blur as time elapsed. During the '60s it was given another life again and afterward the '70s achieved a resurgence of the old ability. In any case, its ubiquity melted away again during the '80s.

However Macramé was nearly turning into a past, it recovered its name when the 21st century saw the presentation of wall decorations, material articles, comforters, little pants shorts, decorative liners, curtains, plant holders and other furniture-related merchandise.

Today, Macramé's ability and side interest implies numerous things to many individuals; in many regards, the ability is phenomenal and remarkable, despite the fact that for other people, it doesn't make any difference. Macramé includes binds the circles to balance out the body and legs. It tends to be extremely unwinding and restorative to the body, psyche and soul to make a macramé item; it's likewise a harmless to the ecosystem workmanship decision. Which are only a portion of the benefits to its specialists that macramé workmanship sweethearts discover this artistic expression bestows.

Utilization of Netted pots for magnificence and common sense in Egypt

Rope-production in Egypt was amazingly evolved from however right on time as this may be not normally refered to in Macramé's texts, yet could well be the absolute first illustration of exquisite bunch tying. Everything began with a bunch A bunch is a fundamental course of uniting two remaining details and associating them. We never pay a qualm to the system, however there is quite a lot more to a bunch. Since the soonest people, hitches have been a customary buddy of humanity who utilized it in useful application and regularly made it into mysterious, logical, religious, clinical, innovative and ornamental things. Macramé is one situation where the fundamental demonstration of bunch tying was transformed into a work of art by man.

The delicacy of material antiquities is an overwhelming test excavator face-they deteriorate a long time before we can uncover them to inspect and record. It was similar issue with the recognizable proof of the Macramé beginnings. Specialists unhesitatingly accept that since man's requirement for building and work developed, tying has been with humankind. The most seasoned apparent occasions of discovering ties were dated somewhere in the range of 15,000 and 17,000 BC. They gauge, however, the hitching could be 250,000 years of age or even existed 2,500,000 years prior.

Beginning and dissemination of present day macramé in the Middle East during thirteenth century

Moreover, the Crusaders who vanquished the Middle East somewhere in the range of 1095 and 1228 additionally came into contact with the workmanship, and it is assumed that their companions and house cleaners who were going with them had taken in this expertise from local people.

While today we consider macramé as enhancing workmanship, its underlying foundations have been more utilitarian than beautifying in nature. This shortsighted type of square tying, otherwise known as macramé, was utilized by Arab weavers to get the last details of their woven items. Macramé is generally liked by ladies these days, as other fiber makes, however not many of the extremely noticeable and fruitful Macrameers were no other than men — mariners, accurately. Understanding the flexibility of the straightforward reef hitch (or otherwise called a square bunch) and furthermore the force of different snare bunches to tie sails and fill payload with the ropes, the early voyagers of oceanic found that tying the bunches could likewise assuage their fatigue. Such mariners additionally began tying for quite a long time adrift, consolidating progressively many-sided hitches into exquisite plans for intermittent utilitarian applications, for example, rope stepping stools and ringer pulls. As the boats moored at various ports, frequently the mariners would sell or deal their items, and Macramé 's craftsmanship — and advancement of such nautical items like twine and rope — began to spread to numerous countries, including China.

The Queen fixated by Lace (seventeenth century, Netherlands and Great Britain)

Mary II was first presented to Macramé in the Netherlands (30 April 1662 – 28 December 1694), because of her union with William of Orange. Both King and Queen shared a propensity for trim. In addition to the fact that she continued to enhance her attire with ribbon, however she likewise made different styles of trim, including Macramé, and showed her women the craft of Macramé in pausing. She is perceived by the British court for carrying Macramé to the women, where it turned into a standard specialty. Sovereign Charlotte was another Royal woman who esteemed macramé. She was responsible for improving the imperial home, and her Macramé ribbon plans were managed into a considerable lot of the goods. She constructed the pattern in Georgian England for Macramé, which at last turned into a famous past-time.

Ireland's Gift to American Macramé History in 1864

The most notable of silk string makers, Barbour from Ireland, shown up in Paterson, New Jersey, during 1864. This made the string most generally utilized for Macramé promptly accessible to the US market.

Sleep years and the Macramé restoration

There came when the Macramé of the Victorian time frame everything except disappeared for over a long time from conventional making methods. During a 1940's distribution, there are little references of the craftsmanship, so it is protected to accept that the rationings and deficiencies of the universal conflicts might have affected this workmanship much as they had on another comparable weaving. This, accordingly, didn't need the more sensible uses of sewing or sewing for some sort of embellishing workmanship. Females likewise joined the assistance when individuals were battling in the universal conflicts. The nonconformity of the 1960s restored Macramé as well as other craftsman specialties like leatherwork, copper work, sewing, and so forth as they defied mechanical assembling and automation.

Chapter 2: Benefits Of Macramé

You can find in this section how indoor plants and the Macramé will assist you with feeling much improved. Houseplants are incredible for your wellbeing, yet what does Macramé have to do with that? All house plants and macramé furnish us with visual allure and quieting results, and together they look incredible. This is likewise an awesome method to bring life into a boring dim space. Truth be told, houseplants do the opposite of what we do while relaxing: transmit oxygen and burn-through carbon dioxide. In addition to the fact that this freshens up the climate, however it likewise eliminates harmful toxins. NASA's broad work has shown that, in 24 hours, houseplants will dispense with up to 87 percent of air poisons. Examination has shown that indoor plants can improve center and efficiency (up to 15 percent!), lower strain rates and lift the mentality — making them ideal for the home as well as for your work environment. Macramé is a striking enhancement decision that helps another plant look remarkable in a room.

At home, at the recreation center, in the nursery or at school, plants are placed in a macramé holder or on the work area, they can assist with adjusting dampness and raise energy rates — encountering vegetation and nature causes one to feel more great and tranquil, which essentially works on the regular mind-set. Indoor plants have a utilitarian and exquisite capacity, introduce a beautiful plant holder with macramé, and it will change and enhance your reality.

Actual Health Benefits

The indoor nursery can be your haven from the external climate, and it is a wellspring of gigantic joy for some individuals. In the event that you stay in a little room or a major house by joining such plants into your family, you will start to see wellbeing and witness charming and fulfilling changes. Utilizing various shades of macramé plant holders will work on the general allure of your nursery room, living space, inside, and decks outside. Together, plants and macramé will work on the temperament and assemble a lounge that is quieting to live in, which can likewise assist with detachment and gloom: really focusing on a living being gives us an explanation and is fulfilling — particularly when you see a delightful macramé plant holder sprouting and prospering in area.

Youth partake in the example as it energizes diverse decisions and makes the very admittance to them to build excellent plans that they are anxious to use for showing at some appropriate chance to their companions. We as a whole love making select pieces, anklets looking like wristbands and groups of fortitude that we may make available for purchase or as giveaways and presents.

Macramé styles, like anklets and wristbands, are incredible for summer wear. They are not just ideal for specific things that are extraordinary yet in any event, for the water. They are truly basic enough for ladies and young ladies of any age as they will discover it very simple to wrap up making the delightful Macramé enriching things.

It is the first run through the Flower Power bunch has got things right. There is a wellbeing acquire in the blossoms and green plants that go with your kids. A good method to raise blossoms and plants is to plant them in pots and hang some utilizing plant holders produced using Macramé.

The Macramé plant holders give ideal ideas to a plan project or a natively constructed present for a companion. The workmanship is so easy to do in just a single day or simply a large portion of a day. Kids should be urged to work on making Macramé projects.

The craftsmanship turned out to be so normal in the seventies that it would adorn almost everybody's patios with Macramé holders in changing tones, and utilizing explicit styles in Macramé ropes. Moreover, plant holders were not difficult to be seen holding indoor plants in the lounge area and kitchen, with huge windows opening to the patio, empowering the cool wind in.

How precisely do Macramé plant holders help your wellbeing? It just so happens, indoor plants, aside from being normal home enrichments, give numerous medical advantages.

Regardless, plants transmit the imperative oxygen; eliminate poisons and carbon dioxide; tidy up the VOCs created by textures, cover filaments, paint and other development materials that trigger wiped out making condition, migraines, sore, dry throats, dry or irritated skin and weakness; assist individuals with mending quicker from infection; and build up a more quiet and really loosening up climate.

As per research embraced by NASA, giving indoor plants wipes out up to 96 percent of carbon monoxide from a room each day. Many plants are considered to dispose of certain unsafe contaminations from the climate, for instance, formaldehyde. You will experience this amazingly unsafe toxin in a wide range of sudden regions, like another floor covering or plastic upholstery. Making of Macramé plant holders or offering one as a gift frequently advances planting indoor plant culture. What more liberal gift will you offer in your home to friends and family than the improvement of a better climate? There could be no other reasonable method of bringing indoor plants into the home than with some refreshed, current Macramé holders.

Macramé ropes or strings are likewise accessible in various shadings. Foster new, current looking plans that carry tone and class to each house, and offer medical advantages to everybody.

Keep in mind, when you make or make Macramé plant holders for your home or as gifts, you are not just making a plain plant holder. In all actuality by enjoying this movement, you advance wellbeing and give joy to the friends and family. It is an endowment of wellbeing and satisfaction for the home. Remembering that, it's an ideal opportunity to get hold of your Macramé ropes and begin hitching.

Creating for Mental Health

Since the start of recorded history, mankind has been captivated with the issue of what is a craftsmanship. The goal of craftsmanship for Tolstoy was to have a way of comprehension among ourselves as well as other people; additionally a method for the Anaïs Nin to purge whatever enthusiastic abundance we might have. Notwithstanding, the best achievement in imagination might be something that can accommodate the two: a passage to understanding into our mind that helps us to both scrub and genuinely like our feelings — that is, a sort of treatment. Macramé has developed and expanded in ubiquity. This is only an aftereffect of the innovative cycle that happens on numerous stages. Alongside experts, novice macramé specialists consider it unwinding, agreeable, creative and fulfilling. For the individuals who simply need to utilize and like the completed things, there is an immense range of alternatives for wonderful macramé to coordinate with the plan of your home, individual style and the closet. Today, Macramé's side interest and the ability mean numerous things to many individuals; in specific regards, the mastery is fabulous and exceptional, despite the fact that for other people, it truly doesn't make any difference. Macramé comprises of tying the bunches that will assist you with settling the arms and hands. Macramé can be truly unwinding and restorative to the body. It additionally relieves the brain and soul to make a macramé item; it's likewise a naturally maintainable craftsmanship decision. These are a couple of the benefits for its specialists.

Notwithstanding the few oddity articles and important things macramé makes, there are many benefits coming about because of the macramé. It is basically restorative. Making things happen and controlling them settles hands and the body. Macramé likewise cultivates the releasing of joints. A few group consider that Macramé is a craft of redundant bunches which are utilized to construct designs is thoughtful, and carries agreement and unwinding to mind.

Many twines and some straightforward bunches are all that a specialist needs to find the colossal potential outcomes that are introduced by macramé. Macramé workmanship doesn't utilize a great deal of materials or hardware.

The strategy known as macramé is the act of hitching numerous assortments of mathematical shapes without requiring the utilization of needles, circles, or snares.

Macramé information and workmanship existed in the thirteenth century. This term macramé, is initially Arabic and signifies "periphery." Arabian weavers are accepted to have started the procedure by hitching extra material to edges of loamed fiber. With such roots during the right on time of the fourteenth and the fifteenth centuries, Macramé at long last made it into Italy and France. Mariners chose to begin rehearsing Macramé in light of the fact that it was a serious fun approach to spend the extended periods of time adrift. Primary bunches utilized by mariners are the simple macramé hitches ... the square bunch, half-hitch tie and furthermore the half bunch. Numerous mariners disseminated their craft to Chinese who applied the procedures to their exceptional culture and human advancement. During the nineteenth century, the ability was mainstream with likewise the British.

The information tumbled to disappointment as time elapsed. It was resuscitated during the 1960s and the 1970s, carrying revitalization to old abilities. Its prevalence reduced during the 1980s and 1990s, yet during the start of the 21st century saw its fruitful re-visitation of its maximum capacity, with a boundless number of imaginative opportunities for specialists, planners, and appreciators of many shifted macramé things.

The craftsmanship and ability in macramé these days group as a type of various things to the various people. In a few cases, ability is brilliant for some. The interfacing of an assortment of bunches can further develop arms and hands. The formation of a macramé task will loosen up the body, brain and soul a considerable amount! Macramé adventures need negligible hardware and include materials without exhaust or synthetic substances; it is absolutely a basic, earth-accommodating expertise.

Meanings of plans can change from the macramé adornments and plant holder's macramé and home assistants to the divider holders for satchels and belts. Macramé's various shades and surfaces take into consideration an expansive reach to pick from. Materials differ from explicit hemp and jute thicknesses to twine, polyester filaments and colored nylon. Not exclusively would you be able to have those wooden globules in the plans, in any case, these days, both ceramic and glass dots are being coordinated into plans. Like different gadgets, workmanship can extend our capabili

Macramé and its ties to the benefits of tying knots

Tying hitches is everything except invigorating. In case you're endeavoring to lock a heap on a truck, fixing kids' bands, doing combating twist hair or attaching a necktie: all the exhausting stuff like that need fixation, accuracy and fine engine abilities. This is additionally a segment of the movement to support development. Bunches are viewed as remedial, unwinding or imaginative, for a decent reason.

While in antiquated history, the act of hitching the ties began as a prerequisite, the present bunches have taken on new importance and importance. There is a wave in DIY and its focal point macramé.

Reappearing in the wake of encountering a second during the 1970s, the present macramé jumps closely following the development toward moderation and care. It's unpreventable via online media, and the art is encouraging the making of fruitful and useful organizations.

Macramé's restoration might make a few group need to mold themselves a noose, however the specialty world, high on sentimentality, is occupied with rehashing screwy, hand-hitched owls and sweet plant holders once contained in radical sacks.

The simple demonstration of associating the bunch quiets you down, rouses you, and assists you with foregetting everything. It is an old and imposing expertise. There is an appealing thing in the present developing innovative climate about making things the hard way and using old methods. Macramé has had a fantastic resurgence, particularly in Canberra.

There are reports of youngsters who have proceeded to work prosperous organizations since dominating the macramé.

However, Macramé is something other than business, it's treatment. Tying ties mitigates. This dials back the heart and digestion, which calms nervousness. This is a spatial capacity that can help those with diseases like Parkinson's, as it is advantageous for smoothness and the sensory system.

While arising developments smooth out our lives, certain regular painstaking work breakdown by the wayside. At the point when the quantity of people using the old fashioned hitching framework lessens, there are others that endeavor to guarantee that such blurring strategies don't disintegrate.

It's likewise useful in exploring profession. Exploring gives youngsters the gifts they need to dominate throughout everyday life and foster resilience to the deterrents they experience throughout everyday life. You gain proficiency with the correspondence characteristics to succeed when you're being instructed as a scout. However, you'll start by figuring out how to tie a modest bunch. Many might see tie tying as an old craftsmanship, yet grown-ups utilize the bunches and abilities they get as youngster scouts.

The specialty of tying the ties and other customary artworks are surely expected to endure for an extremely long period in the web time where individuals can share their abilities by clicking a tick. You simply need to follow the string, and you can wind up in improbable areas.

Advantages of Macramé Plant Hanger

Today Macramé plant holder is the vogue. The new pattern can be followed back to Macramé's numerous properties, including its association with nature, complexity, and advantageous wellbeing sway. A macramé plant holder is regular craftsmanship. It really doesn't permit synthetic substances to be utilized. More customers worldwide have come to comprehend the benefit of making and buying naturally feasible items. Plant holder is basically binds bunches to make imaginative and impeccable bits of workmanship that are utilized to feature plants at home. It offers you different approaches to flaunt your plants. A macramé plant holder is an ideal spot to show your plants. You can't overlook the normal tastefulness that shows up in homes where this superb piece of craftsmanship is utilized with various types of plants and compartments. They will keep going for such countless years whenever made eagerly. You should put the pruned plants in the holder to offer the wonderful, normal feel.

A few residents take the craft of a Macramé plant holder as a pastime. They regularly accept it as a method of achieving monetary freedom. Did you at any point consider that this craftsmanship allows you the opportunity to practice your body? Then, at that point, you have next to no materials to utilize that lessen the challenges related with these artworks. To deliver this specialty, one requirements zero force supply use.

Whenever and on quickly, the Macramé plant holder is an incredible present. This will likewise be recalled by your friends and family on the grounds that the awesome present is carefully assembled. You realize we have begun to embrace and like the artworks made manually.

Prosperity

In our current reality where such a large amount our capacity is undetectable, where occupations and culture are on occasion isolated, and where examination happens on PCs and in the computerized world; making stuff with our hands and fingers works with a sensation of force and matchless quality. This is a method of building substantial concordance and style – a genuine tangible touch point – and getting once again into our dynamic grown-up lives a sensation of open and agreeable play. To such an extent, that numerous experts are rapidly reassuring weaving as a restorative practice. The world has started to understand that these artworks make a similar restorative encounter, be it sewing, stitching, weaving, or Macramé.

Macramé is incredibly helpful

Specialists highlight the Relaxation Response: the cadenced rehashed movements will in general place us in the current second, loosening up our heads, which are too regularly brimming with action and stresses, and the examination shows that such rehashed signals give a solid alleviating impact – including coming from our hands and going from one side to another with our understudies.

Weaving requires a convoluted, synchronous and synchronized move cycle and it makes a great deal of mind energy, which guarantees that the cerebrum has less an ideal opportunity to focus on specific things, and it's an ideal quieting procedure for those with industrious torments. Also, the rehashed action utilized with weaving expands serotonin creation, which might cause us to turn out to be more loose and more joyful. The musical part of the movements is alleviating, which adds to a condition of examination.

Sewing will take you to quiet, actually, place where the example and join are all that you can focus on. You can encounter the yarn's thickness and see the clear tones, hear the needles continually turning, and simultaneously with your ideal plan and the result you will have a sensation of accomplishment. You will distinguish the different smells of the fleece of every single regular goat. As the entirety of that is heard, time seems to quit going. Your feelings of trepidation are steadily slipping further. What's more, when you complete a thing, the mind-boggling sensation of achievement is top notch.

Health advantages

Through her exploration, a notable psychotherapist found that there was as yet a lack of a whole individual way to deal with clinical treatment through mental practice and that the pattern of certified recuperation exudes from profound inside the brain and soul and will occur despite the fact that a 'fix' isn't accessible.

Remedial turning ought to be a guide to upgrade wellbeing and health. It will uphold people who have torment, melancholy and other psychological well-being issues.

Sewing additionally interfaces us

Among the other actual wellbeing impacts, like turning into a pain killer and stress reliever, weaving frequently ties you to an informal community and individual knitter's companions, and this is especially pertinent for any individual who feels alone, disappointed and forlorn. Knitters make relics that individuals appreciate. You can perk up like a knitter by stroking fleece. Weaving and sewing is the one basic helpful and quieting gadget that you should convey with you all over the place – you get significant serenity and an excellent scarf.

Ply yarns magnificence into your life!

Chapter 3: Macramé Toolbox

Macramé Materials

Macramé beauticians utilize various kinds of materials. The materials can be arranged in two significant manners: normal materials and engineered materials.

Regular Materials

The characteristics of normal materials contrast from manufactured material and realizing these characteristics would assist you with utilizing them. Regular string materials existing today incorporate jute, hemp, calfskin, cotton, silk, and flax. There are additionally yarns produced using regular filaments. Normal material strands are produced using plants and creatures.

Manufactured Materials

As normal materials, engineered materials are additionally utilized in macramé projects. The strands of manufactured materials are made through compound cycles. The significant ones are nylon, beading, line, olefin, glossy silk string, and parachute rope.

Cord Measurement

Before you can set out on a macramé project, it is fundamental that you decide the measure of string you will require. This incorporates knowing the length of the necessary rope and the materials you need to buy.

Estimating Width

The primary thing to do is to decide the completed width of the broadest space of your task. When you have this width, pencil it down.

Then, decide the genuine size of the materials, by estimating its width from one edge to another.

You would then be able to continue to decide the sort of bunch design you wish to use with the information on the bunch design. You should know the width and dividing (whenever expected) of each bunch. You ought to likewise decide whether you need to add more strings to augment a region, or on the other hand in the event that you would require additional lines for damps. With the recipe given above, ascertain and decide the boundary of the ring of your plans.

Decide the mounting method to be utilized. The string can be mounted to a dowel, ring, or other line. Collapsed strings influence both the length and width of the line estimation.

Line Preparation

Line Preparation is a subject once in a while found in books on Macrame. The main advance for any Macrame project is to set up the line tips appropriately. Materials may likewise should be adapted or rigidised.

This shows you distinctive approaches to deal with the cut closures, to keep the ropes from unwinding while you are working. Material taking care of can cause closes that are chaotic and frayed which can be baffling. Wound materials are probably going to crumble totally, except if you take care of business BEFORE beginning your venture.

The getting ready of the strings will occur when each is cut, which is typically the principal stage.

Molding

You can apply beeswax to mellow it after you cut each line from the roll, and wipe out any vapor. Warmth up the wax in your palms, then, at that point spread it like a colored pencil, scouring it down the line length (the two sides). It is prescribed that you apply beeswax to every single normal material (aside from cowhide) or a comparable item. Beeswax can be added to Satin and fine Nylon Beading strings by using Organic Materials. The others are positive.

Following preparing of the strings, genuinely take a look at each for defects. Dispose of any harmed material. Then, at that point, utilizing one of the accompanying string care strategies:

Getting ready with Tape

"Quarrel" infers eliminating the strands. So the utilization of tape to hold the strands together is one method that can be utilized to get ready ropes. Cut a piece of SMALL covering tape (or a cellophane tape). Fold it over the string's tip while pressing the region to limit it up.

You might manage the locale with the tape all through the completing system. That is my principle procedure and when I add dots I use it. By making the tip limited and as level as could be expected, the section of the string through the dab is a lot simpler.

Planning with Knots

One quick and simple approach to plan ropes is to tie ties near tips. One choice is the Overhand Knot.

The bunch in Figure 8 is another choice. It's easy to tie and eliminate. This is the most ideal choice for adaptable strings, where eventually you need to eliminate the bunches. It won't get as close as different bunches.

When working with tricky material, like Satin or Nylon, utilize the Stevedore Knot. You can put it on a string anyplace, and it is extremely simple to tie.

Getting ready with Glue

There are sure paste marks uniquely figured to forestall fraying of the lines. Paste works best with 1mm-to 3mm-wide ropes. Prior to utilizing it, you should test the paste on a little piece of material to check whether there is harm. A few brands will diminish the material for all time. Family cement may likewise be utilized to clean strings. First weaken it with water, then, at that point toss the finishes into the cement.

You should move the tips between the fingertips in designs where you plan to connect dots and make them more modest, as the cement is drying. Nail clean ought to regularly be utilized in a similar way, spreading it with the brush or by scouring.

Getting ready with a Flame

Engineered materials can now and then be ready and completed from a BBQ lighter with a fire. This technique ought to get ready Parachute rope ALWAYS. Ensure that you first test the material, by applying a fire to a little piece. The material requirements to MELT as opposed to consuming. The dissolved part of the material will be more obscure than the rest, yet ought NOT touch off.

Olefin, Polyester, and Nylon ought to be ready as follows:

Hold the fire for 1 to 5 seconds at the rope's tip, then, at that point stop when the region is liquefied.

Significant: Watch the rope for consuming signs, and stop when you see it light.

Planning Parachute Cord (Paracord)

Parachute rope is fairly unique, since it comprises of a few center yarns encompassed by a twisted sleeve. In the principle yarns you need to cover by consuming the sleeve around them or you risk accidentally taking them out when you're running. The rope then, at that point assemble, or totally break.

Here's the manner by which you plan Paracord:

• Pull the center yarns out of the sleeve following cutting, so you uncover around 1/2-inch.

• Rip back the primary yarns, and that the external coat is on.

• Instead move the external sleeve in, so you can presently don't see the primary yarns.

• Apply the fire to the external sleeve, until MELT is apparent. Then, at that point press the BBQ lighter handle down onto the space and smooth it quite far.

The dissolved region will look similar as plastic, and the material will be more obscure.

Finishing Techniques

Completing methods are explicit beautifying bunches and techniques which are utilized in the last strides of Macrame tasks to deliver a perfect appearance.

To portray this interaction the term TIE OFF is regularly utilized. I'm alluding to those methods in this present site's free examples, and you'll likewise think that they are in most Macrame books.

1. Completing Knots

In many Macrame designs the Overhand bunch is much of the time utilized in the last advances. You'll more often than not be tying this completing bunch with two strings.

You might have to make an Overhand Knot with just one line once in a while. You make a circle clockwise way, then, at that point from beneath (under-finished) go through the end.

Paste is regularly used to finish ties, since they stay secure. Texture stick is the best sort to utilize yet it likewise functions admirably with family stick. Simply ensure CLEAR dries out. INSIDE the bunch is the best spot to apply stick not long before you fix it as far as possible.

When utilizing completing bunches in an undertaking, have a go at setting them where they aren't appearing. I utilized the Overhand Knot in this picture of the Square Knot Frame to tie two strings at the rear of the edge.

The Barrel Knot is one more famous bunch to wrap up. Over the long haul, it's less adept to break and you don't have to apply cement. This shows 2 strings connected in the bunch. With one line it appears to be unique yet the guidelines are something similar (beneath).

Stage 1

• Start the Barrel Knot by making an Overhand bunch.

• Move the end around and through the circle a subsequent time.

Stage 2

The most ideal approach to make a neatly completed glance toward the finish of a rope is to add a dot prior to appending the completing bunch. This strategy capacities well by using globules and string materials created from Micro-Macrame.

The finishes had gone through a dab in the Oval Bracelet. An Overhand bunch was tied, and afterward the finishes, a contrary way, went through once more. Paste was added to the tie, and the globule was pushed to the tip. When it was dry, the closures close to the dot were cut off.

2. Collapsing Techniques

Straightforward collapsing strategies, similar to those displayed beneath, are astounding completing procedures for some activities in Macrame. The technique you pick relies upon the kind of line material with which you work, and how adaptable it is.

Adaptable materials, for example, cotton will effortlessly crease the closures level against the back surface of the article you're making. You then, at that point apply the cement to hold them set up under the closures, keeping them level as it dries.

A further stage can include the utilization of less adaptable materials:

• Fold the strings to the back, then, at that point pass at least one bunches under a circle.

• Add glue and require the abundance content to fix until it is eliminated.

You might have to utilize fine tip forceps, careful clips, or tweezers while going through the finishes under circles. From one bunch you move the gadget under the ring, keep the edge, then, at that point acquire it. You might even Loop the finishes in the example across spaces yet just if the ties lay close together.

Trim the finishes prior to weaving, to prune them however much as could be expected. Then, at that point use forceps or tweezers to weave each end in the overall region, over and under a few spaces. In the event that the ties are past one another you can not see the closures. On the off chance that they don't mix in, utilize one of the other completing procedures.

3. Getting done with Fringe

Periphery making is one of Macrame's most normal completing methods.

The articulation Macrame is gotten from the Arabic word "Miqrama" that can be changed over into fancy periphery.

You have two alternatives: You can assemble a Brushed Fringe or a Beaded Fringe. Brushed periphery, similar to this Snow Owl, is frequently utilized in Macrame creatures. As you find in this image (top of the head), you might brush each fiber totally smooth. Another alternative is to disentangle the lines and permit the strands to stay wavy, as displayed in the wing feathers here.

Sometimes you might be approached to make a brushed periphery formed, so it follows the point of the bunches from which the ropes come. This picture shows the Owl Holder's tail feathers, which are cut at a point. Beaded Fringe is one of my #1 completing procedures. Isolating the strings into at least two gatherings is the way to making it look great. Then, at that point you will deliver the periphery, which is not so much cumbersome but rather more engaging, on different stages.

The Royal Hanger looks extraordinary with a beaded periphery layered on it. The long periphery is produced using a couple of ropes that come from inside the group. Then, at that point you make the more limited periphery with the excess strings that encompass the others (the lines outside).

• You might utilize 9 mm glass crow rollers for the 3 mm-4 mm size content, as found in this Two Tone Planter.

• 12 mm wood barrel dots (5 mm openings) are proper for 5 mm-6 mm content.

This Fringed Table has a beaded molded periphery at the top and base underneath the V formed plans. The periphery fits the point of V arrangement by gauging each harmony and situating the globules at a similar distance under each bunch.

Difference Between A String SA Rope And A Cord

Macramé string is a smooth, single contort string like the one Niroma Studio has gotten popular for.

String extends quicker than string since it loosens up rapidly so the absolute width will go from 1 to 1.5 mm, from when solidly injured along the channel to while parting and breathable. Different retailers may call it something else, however, so remember that.

"What's the right macramé string for novices?"

I generally get addressed, and I generally pick the 5 mm regular cotton string. It is the right size to hang in a decent medium-sized divider, and it fits better compared to the 3 mm; also, it has an extremely conservative medium wind on it, and it very well may be tenderly unknotted and two or multiple times prior to losing its flexibility as long as you are cautious. Also, being delicate on the hands, obviously, consistently will in general keep you moving!

Macramé rope is ordinarily a 3-strand rope where the filaments are folded over one another (occasionally called a 3-handle). You may likewise think that it is in four strands, however the customary rope will be three strands. Macramé rope is generally more grounded than macramé string, and it gives you a flawless, wavy periphery when you untwist it, so it's ideally suited for adding measurement to your work.

Since it is heavier, I like to utilize it for parts of things that convey extensive weight. Macramé rope regularly extends when it has been cut, so relying upon where you stay, how much moistness you have, and so on, it will likewise extend up to 1 cm.

Macramé rope is normally a 6-strand (or more) interlaced string, for sure I accept was all the more broadly utilized for macramé during the 1970s to mid 1980s when the cotton string wasn't by and large 'what' to utilize. The firmly woven cotton macramé rope is at times called "band rope." Sash rope is marginally unbending to utilize and very difficult to eliminate, yet it's superb, so it's ideal for weight-bearing parts and in case you're attempting to add a lot of solidarity to your work. I would say, macramé rope is the most exceedingly awful on hands, however you should manage the slight uneasiness when you need a specific look or flexibility.

Then, at that point, polypropylene (or polyolefin) macramé rope is ideally suited for open air use since it doesn't lose its shape as fast as cotton. Nonetheless, the edges can look "crimped," so that is the lone thing to remember.

Tools Required For Macramé

Beside Kumihimo, hitching and interlacing strategies require minimal in the method of specific gear; truth be told, most beavers or craftsmans will presumably as of now have any devices required in their workbox, so you ought to have the option to go straight away. For insights regarding what you need to kick off Kumihimo, allude to Kumihimo: Tools and materials.

Adornments Tools

A basic assortment of three devices to change interlaces or tying into adornments is required. Purchasing great quality, fine devices is consistently advantageous in light of the fact that these will assist you with completing jobs rapidly and proficiently, however stay away from small scale devices in light of the fact that these will make your hands sore when utilized for significant stretches.

Wire Cutters

Pick side cutters, or in a perfect world flushcutters, what slice the wire or headpins to a straight end. Brain to eliminate into the position or to confront away from the tail with the level side of the cutters.

Round-Nose Pliers

These forceps are utilized to make wire or head-pins circles. The jaws are cone-formed, so you can change the circle size by working with little circles close to the highest point of the jaws and for bigger circles close to the base. Frequently work a similar distance downwards to make circles of a similar size.

They are utilized to control wire and headpins or to open and close leap rings. Frequently search for somewhat smooth surfaces within the jaws – pinholes from the nearby tool shop are unsatisfactory as aside from being excessively wide, they are probably going to have profound hold serrations that will harm the metal. Gruff end forceps are the instrument for workhorses, however kill nose pincers (chain-nose) with tightened jaws permit you to draw nearer.

Expert instruments albeit not fundamental, this unit will assist you with expertly completing adornments, so think about contributing if possible.

Bowed Nose Pinions

These are basically kill nose pinions with a right-point twist in the jaws, permitting you to get into abnormal positions and hold wire or headpins as needed at a more agreeable point.

Nylon-Jaw Pliers

These forceps have a gentler material that covers the metal jaws to forestall harm to milder wires and results. They come as round-nose or level nose forceps.

Crease Pliers

Accessible in three sizes-miniature, medium, and large scale these pincers are utilized fundamentally for shutting creases perfectly around dot string. The forceps match the wire thickness and the size of the crease.

Split-Ring Pinions

With a uniquely created tip for split-ring opening, these will positively assist with forestalling broken nails!

Drill

A drill is valuable for moving ropes and meshes through metal finds and facilitating them.

Twist Posts

Cinch over the edge of the outside of work and put a specific distance aside for twisting long rope lengths.

Certain Essentials

These things can put or be found in your tool kit; they will be valuable when hitching and plaiting.

Scissors

Hold a few distinct sorts of scissors rigorously for string and rope cutting and don't utilize them for paper cutting since this would break the edges without any problem. Enormous scissors are appropriate for length cutting of strings and ropes and little scissors with sharp spots are useful for smooth cutting of finishes.

Needles

A wide range of needles can make completing meshes and tying or string dots simpler.

Sewing needles, A bunch of sewing needles of different sizes assists you with sewing through twists or secure closures in the wake of wrapping. Sharps have a minuscule hand, yet they are extremely solid and can be utilized to string little seed globules into harder strings. Weaving needles have longer peered toward to facilitate the stringing.

Woven artwork needles These have a genuinely unpolished tip and an enormous eye and are valuable to string bigger globules onto a string or to control ties set up.

Fine beading needles are utilized to append seed dots and other little globules to the interlaces or to cover joins. Ideal for size 11 seed dabs and size 12 or 13 for size 15 seed dots, a size 10 needle. Keep a decent stock, as the better needles will curve and break specifically.

Turned wire needles by circling the fine wire over the jaws of round-nose pincers and arranging the tails, you can make your own necessities. On the other hand, they can be purchased in an assortment of sizes to circle dabs onto a string or string, or to pull circles or lines to work or neaten closes into twists.

Enormous eye needles. These two-pointed long needles are valuable for hanging globules on multi-strands of fine strings, yet try not to get ropes through a restricted space as the two fine poles that different the needle at the bound end.

Pins

Dressmaker's pins

Helpful for plait stamping at a particular length, separating dabs or embellishments, or situating wrapped strings.

Guide pins

These short pins with ball closes are ideal when working macramé to secure the strings and strings. Fitting it into a corkboard or froth center casing.

Glues

To tie lines and strings and render gems and different frill. Pick the best glue to coordinate with the materials that you stick to, and make sure to leave for 24 hours. Pastes like G-S Hypo Cement and E6000 are made especially for adornments. The paste shapes yet remains flexible, so it is doubtful to break a lot off over the long haul. The G-S Hypo Cement has a fine spout that is reasonable for applying a limited quantity for a smooth completion, then, at that point utilizing a mixed drink stick to apply the paste.

Superglue

These moment pastes can be valuable on the grounds that the material isn't to be left set up before the paste sets. Bound to run the gel adaptation, so it's simpler to be reliable, so add a little volume. Be careful, as these pastes of cyanoacrylate tie skin.

Epoxy pitch

A two-section cement is very appropriate for staying ropes onto metal finds. Wipe off surfaces with a nail clean remover prior to applying the glue to eliminate oily fingerprints. A 5-minute epoxy gum abbreviates drying time, and when utilized, one that dries clear is less inclined to become noticeable.

Beginner Guide To Macrame Cord And Metal Shapes

Knotted string, additionally alluded to as Macrame rope, is the widespread macrame line that you'll discover at your large box retailers, Hobby Lobby, Michaels, and even Wal-shop. Most of macrame amateurs will begin by buying a hitched rope since it is quite possibly the most efficient and furthermore the most helpful strategies to begin macrame. Commonly, it is a twisted rope accessible at most art stores just as enormous box vendors. Many individuals rush to their neighborhood store to get whatever link they can find when they mean to begin today. In the wake of doing a couple of macrame jobs, they will quickly understand the twisted rope isn't the best sort of wire for making macrame. The justification this is on the grounds that the meshed link is for the most part rope made up independently or as a blend of cotton, polyester, polypropylene, or different other strong strands. It's magnificent for connecting things together and furthermore offering it a strong hold, yet is trying to un-tie just as edge with.

So, using a hitched line is anything but a helpless spot to begin. It takes care of business also as you can end up with a mostly nice did job. Normally, you'll end up progressing to either 3-utilize or the most much of the time utilized macrame rope, single hair rope. You may frequently catch wind of utilizing macrame rope just as line. They are for the most part talking about a practically identical thing. The manner in which I put the two aside is that rope is commonly tied or 3-employ rope and link is a sweeping term for strands, string, and even line.

Macrame 3-Ply/3-Stands Cord

3-handle is in like manner depicted as 3-stands line. It is made out of 3 more modest strands in a major bent rope. You will regularly hear macrame experts notice utilizing a 3-employ or 4-handle macrame line, which just means the quantity of hairs turned with one another to foster one single strand of wire. Recorded beneath, you'll have the option to see the qualification between 3-Ply and 4-Ply tastefully.

At the point when you start getting into macrame lines that are more noteworthy than three strands, this is the thing that is portrayed as multi-handle, where you can have 4, 5, or 6-strands, all turned together to make one strand. As should be obvious, there are four hairs wound with one another to foster a solitary hair of rope.

Macrame Single Hair Cord

Singular hair cotton rope is, definitely, the best sort of macrame string to choose from in case you are choosing to get into macrame as an ordinary recreation movement or regular work. Single strand rope is normally much more costly and, accordingly, in the event that you don't wish to overdo it immediately on the expensive link, track down some more affordable cotton rope on Amazon and furthermore start with those. However long it fits on the hands, it will be extraordinary to acquire from. It will without a doubt make it a lot simpler to lessen string, tying ties, unwinding hitches, and bordering the link.

Since you have the data about the three different sorts of macrame line, we should examine four basic focuses that you should search for while figuring out what macrame line to use on your macrame projects.

Macrame Cord Make-Up

Macrame line falls into two parts - All-regular or Synthetic strands. Regular filaments are strands produced in the climate. They are made by plants, creatures, or topographical techniques. Instances of regular strands are cotton, bed cloth, hemp, and fleece, just as hemp. Those filaments can be separated and reused.

The other option is counterfeit filaments. Fake strands are produced using made polymers of little atoms. The substances that utilize these filaments come from important materials, for example, petrol based synthetics or petrochemicals. Instances of manufactured strands are nylon, polyester, and furthermore spandex.

Macrame Cord Texture

On the off chance that you have seen an assortment of such strings, you will find each spool of the link has an alternate inclination, finish, and furthermore appearance to it. Getting a feeling of the different sorts of line surfaces is a fundamental segment of perceiving your macrame lines.

The more macrame pieces you make, the more quickly you'll reveal the surfaces that assume a gigantic part in the entirety of your macrame assignments. In case you will buy the macrame string on the web, attempt different brand name merchants just as see what design fits you. You will positively track down that not all macrame cotton strings are made equivalent. The design, just as feel to the wires, may change from one supplier to the next.

Macrame Cord Size

Realizing the string measurement is in like manner critical while making your ideal macrame work. The part of the rope has a critical impact in the tasteful appearance of macrame projects.

We will not be meticulously describing the situation on macrame line measurements. In case you're intrigued, we do have one more article that audits the different parts of the macrame line. What size of the macrame line do I use for my undertakings? For straightforwardness, the macrame line can be separated directly into three gatherings - little, medium, and enormous.

1.   Little Macrame Cord - is regularly your 1-2 mm breadth string. You'll regularly discover these strings utilized in making valuable gems to string through grains and furthermore switches and little definite specialty occupations.

2.   Medium Macrame Cord - is the place where you will find that most of all macrame projects are made. It is generally between 3mm-5mm. Most of the time, you'll go with 3mm or 4mm. These measurements are broadly utilized for plant holders, inside decorations, lights, wraps, rugs, and so forth

3.   Big Macrame Cord- - This will be your BIG macrame pieces. This will be in the assortment of anything 6mm or more. Regularly, these huge sizes are utilized to cover huge spaces of room. You will find the bunches will in general be less, in any case, significantly bigger.

WHAT CORD DO YOU USE FOR MACRAME?

One of the most clear reactions is: it depends. I would unquestionably suggest utilizing 3mm-4mm Solitary Strand Cotton Cord. On the off chance that you have really endeavored a couple of undertakings utilizing a more affordable string, and you're currently happy with purchasing better wire for top quality positions from that point onward, the single-strand line may be appropriate for you. In case you are a novice, just as need to begin utilizing everything link today then, at that point, obviously, you can do that too.

The motivation behind why I would surely exhort utilizing a singular hair line is that it will further develop your macrame insight. Associating hitches and interpreting them will without a doubt be considerably less of a fight. Cutting ties and bordering won't need to feel like hard work, and furthermore, most prominently, your macrame errands will be satisfying.

Macrame Beginners/Occasional Knotters

I perceive that few out of every odd individual is at a similar stage in their macrame trip, so my reference couldn't matter to each individual. In case you're shiny new to this art, I would surely instruct making use regarding any sort of rope you have lying around to rehearse. Something else, acquire some modest string from your provincial art shop in case you are anxious to start immediately or get some from amazon.com. This string from Amazon is far superior to the link you can discover at your local specialty store. Utilize this string to work on connecting macrame ties, designs just as series. This is the most spending plan well disposed macrame rope to kick you off. Start by making more modest macrame assignments like essential chains or macrame crest examples to figure out making the bunches.

Macrame Lovers and Lovers

For those of you hoping to make your macrame restricting strategies and furthermore to grandstand your assignments, I would prompt top quality 3mm-4mm Single Strand Cotton Cord.

The delicate inclination and accommodation of hitching, close by the simple bordering, makes the absolute best kind of macrame line to use. I use it for almost 100% of my macrame occupations. Bochiknot Macrame gives the top notch macrame cotton string on the web. In case you're planning to begin on macrame errands, one axle of 3mm single strand cotton rope will be a lot of links to get you rolling.

One shaft of macrame line ought to have the option to give you 2 to 3 instrument estimated macrame occupations. In case you're looking for somewhat more, so you don't need macrame line, two axles would without a doubt be all that anyone could need to cover present and future macrame assignments.

Chapter 4: How To Get Started To Macrame – The Basic Knots

Lark's Head Knot

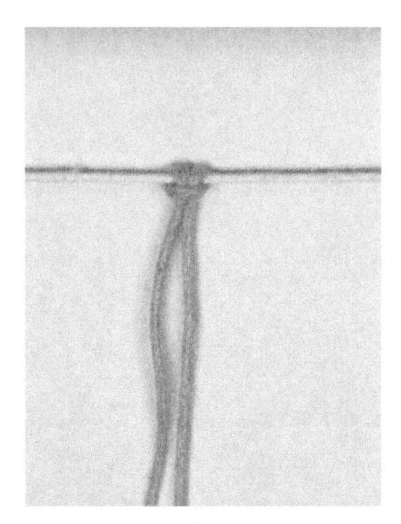

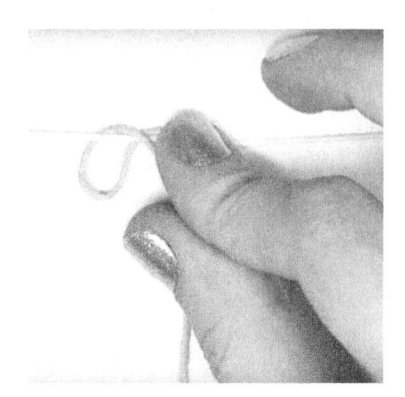

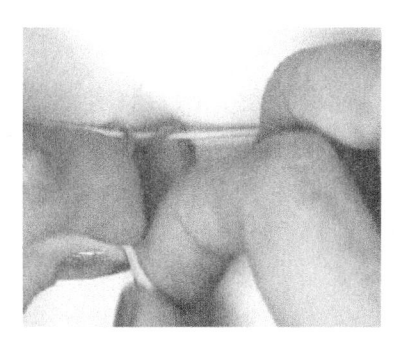

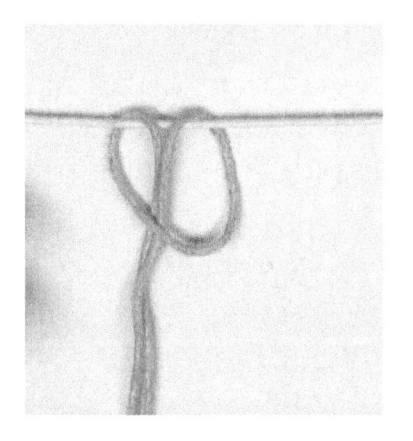

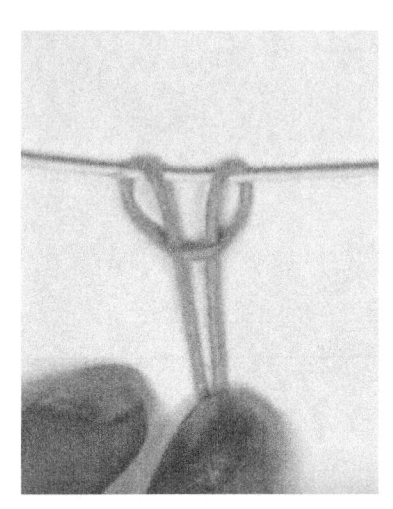

This is an extraordinary starting bunch for any project and can be utilized as the establishment of the task. Utilize a lightweight string for this; it tends to be bought at create stores or on the web, any place you get your macramé supplies.

Watch the photographs cautiously as you move alongside this task and require some investment to ensure you are utilizing the right string, at the right mark of the venture.

Utilize the base string as the center piece of the bunch, working around the finish of the string with the line. Ensure everything is even, as you circle the string around the foundation of the line.

Make a slip tie around the foundation of the string and keep the two closures even as you get the rope through the focal point of the piece.

For the completed task, ensure that you have every one of your bunches secure and firm all through, and put forth a valiant effort to ensure it is all even.

It will take practice before you can get it entirely each time, yet recollect that training makes awesome, and with time, you will get it, without a difficult situation.

Ensure everything is even and secure and tie off. Clip off every one of the remaining details, and you are all set!

Turn around Lark's Head Knot

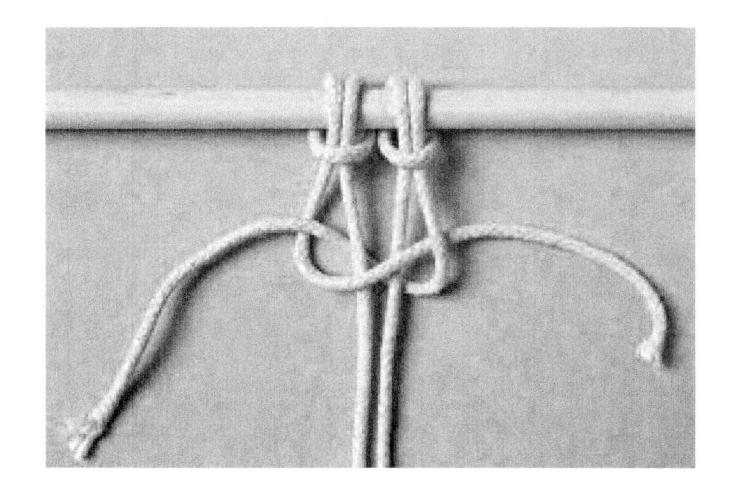

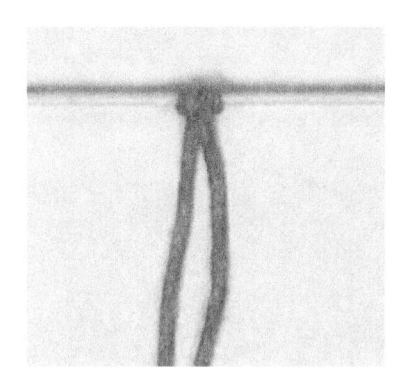

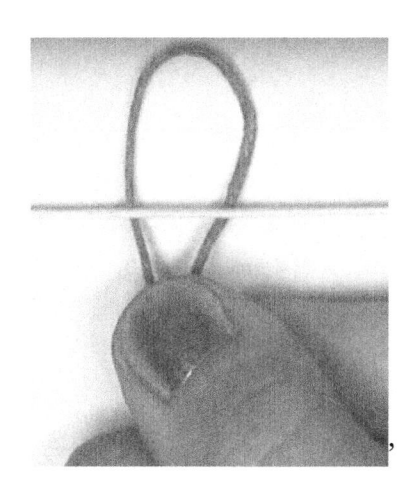

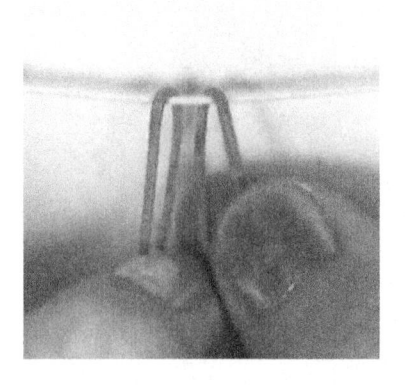

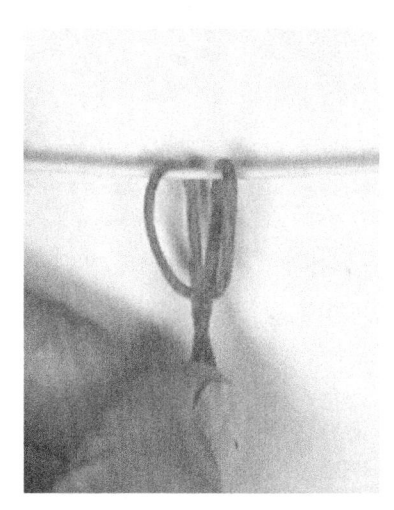

This is an incredible starting bunch and can be utilized as the establishment of the venture. Utilize a lightweight rope for this; this again can be bought at create stores or on the web, any place you get your macramé supplies.

Try not to surge, and ensure you have even strain all through. Careful discipline brings about promising results, however with the delineations to help you, you will discover it isn't hard at all to make.

Utilize two hands to ensure that you have everything even and tight, as you work. You can utilize tweezers in the event that it assists with making it tight against the foundation of the string.

Utilize two hands to pull the string equitably down against the base string to make the bunch.

Once more, keep the base even as you pull the middle, making the firm bunch against your aide line.

For the completed task, ensure that you have every one of your bunches secure and firm all through, and put forth a valiant effort to ensure it is all even. It will take practice before you can get it completely each time, however recollect that training makes awesome, and with time, you will get it without a difficult situation.

Capuchin Knot

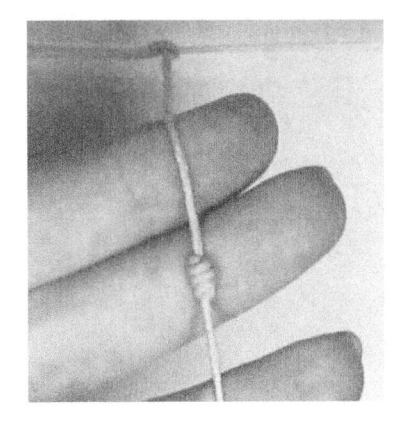

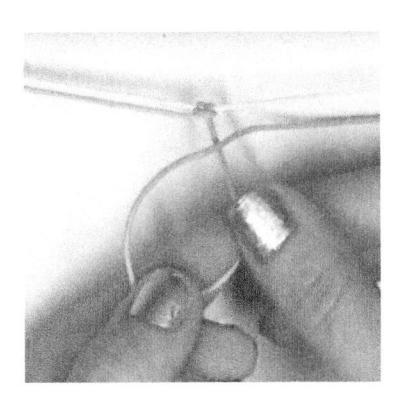

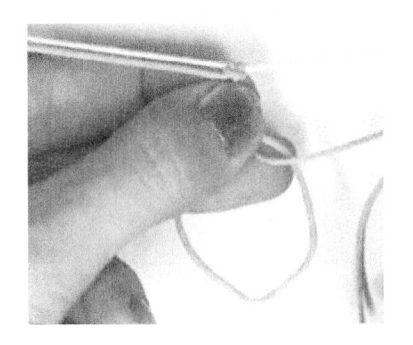

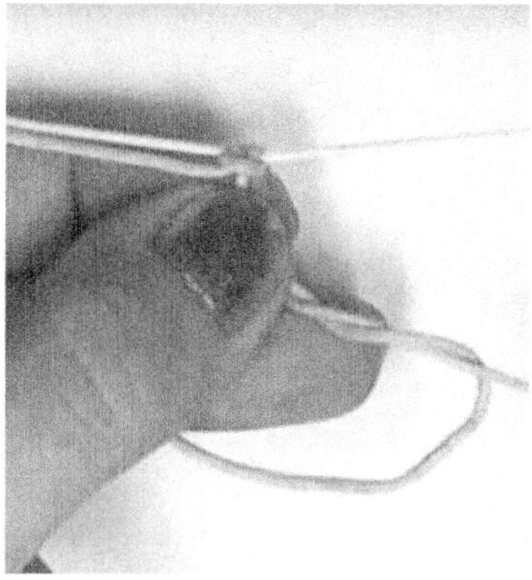

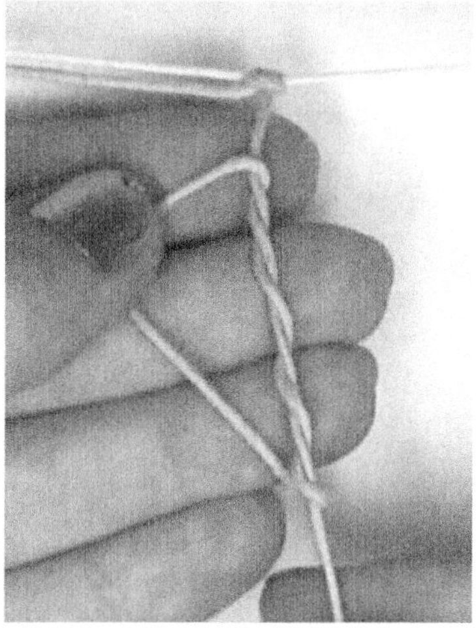

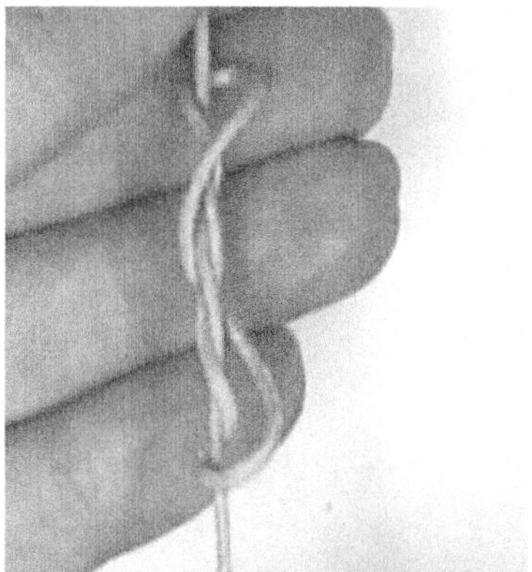

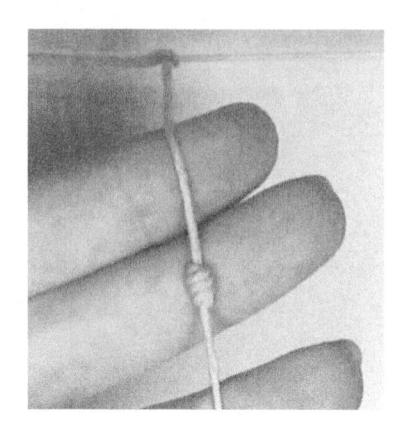

This bunch for any project and can be utilized as the establishment of the venture. Utilize a lightweight string for this.

Watch the photographs cautiously as you move alongside this task and require some investment to ensure you are utilizing the right string, at the right place of the undertaking.

Start with the base rope, securing the bunch onto this, and working your direction alongside the venture. Turn the rope around itself multiple times, getting the string through the middle to frame the bunch. Ensure everything is even and secure and tie off. Clip off every one of the remaining details, and you are all set!

Crown Knot

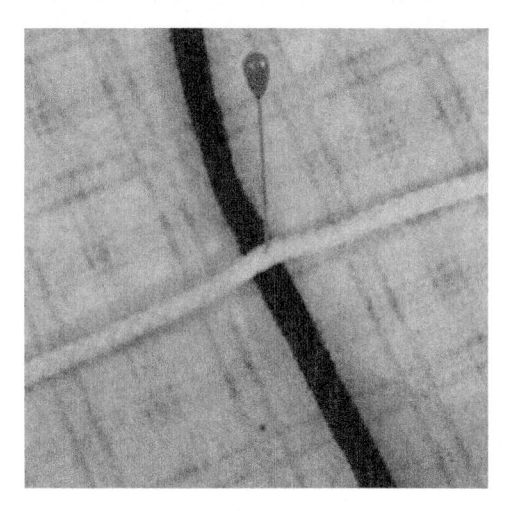

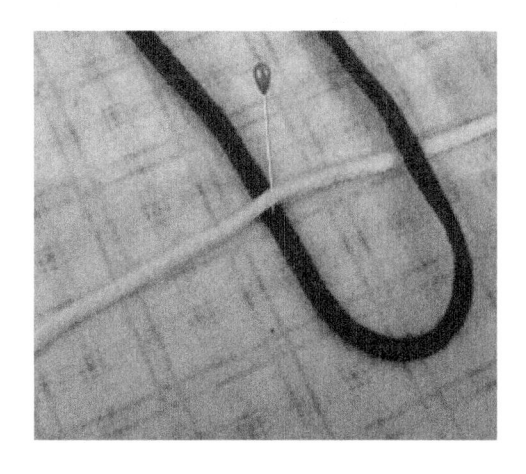

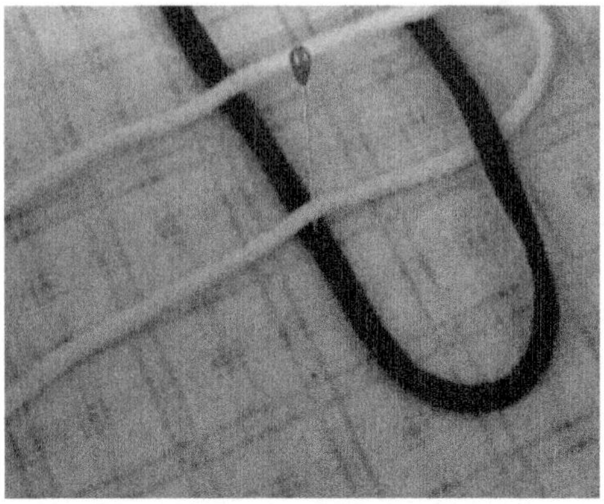

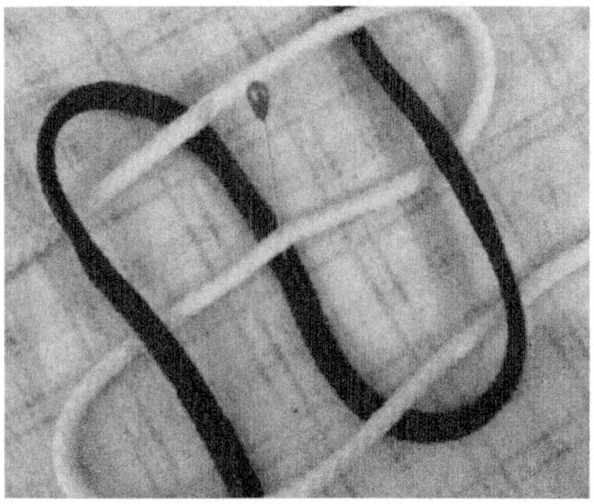

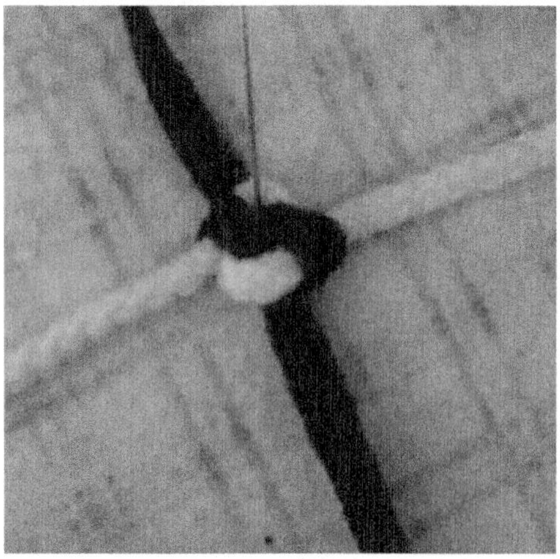

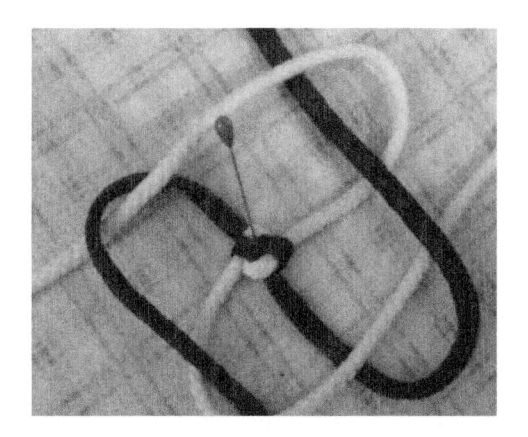

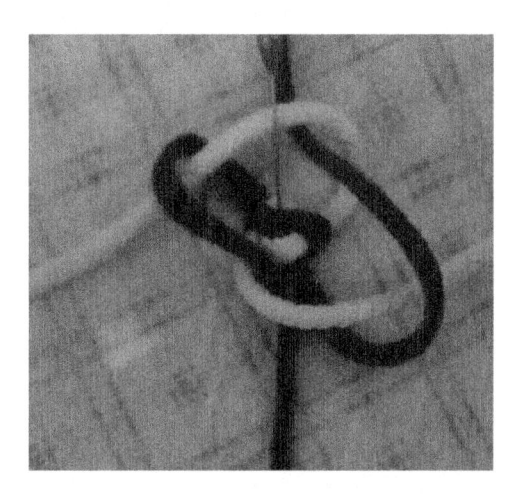

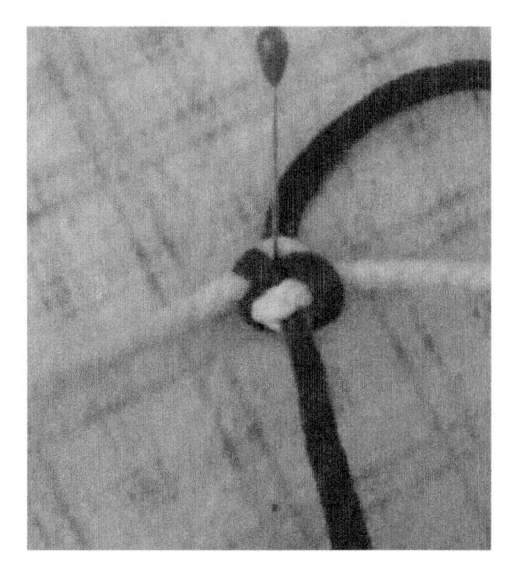

This is an extraordinary starting bunch and can be utilized as the establishment of the task. Utilize a lightweight string for this. Do not surge, and ensure you have even pressure all through. Careful discipline brings about promising results, however with the representations to help you, you will discover it isn't hard at all to make. Utilize a pin to assist with keeping everything set up as you are working. Weave the strings all through one another as you can find in the photographs. It assists with rehearsing with various shadings, to help you see what is happening. Pull the bunch tight, then, at that point rehash for the following column outwardly. Keep on doing this as regularly as you like to make the bunch. You can make it as thick as you prefer, contingent upon the task. You can likewise make more than one length on a similar line. For the completed task, ensure that you have every one of your bunches secure and firm all through, and give a valiant effort to ensure it is all even. Ensure everything is even and secure and tie off. Cut off every one of the last details, and you are all set!

Askew Double Half-tie

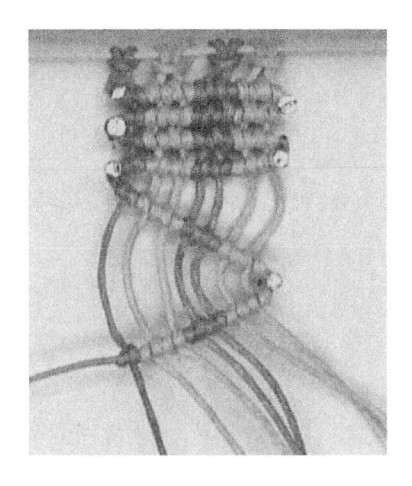

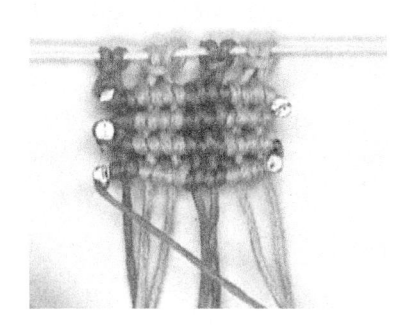

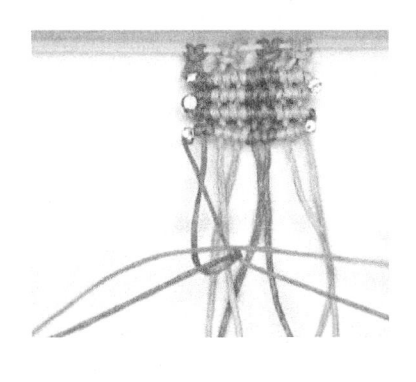

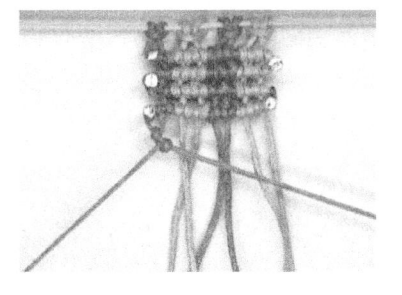

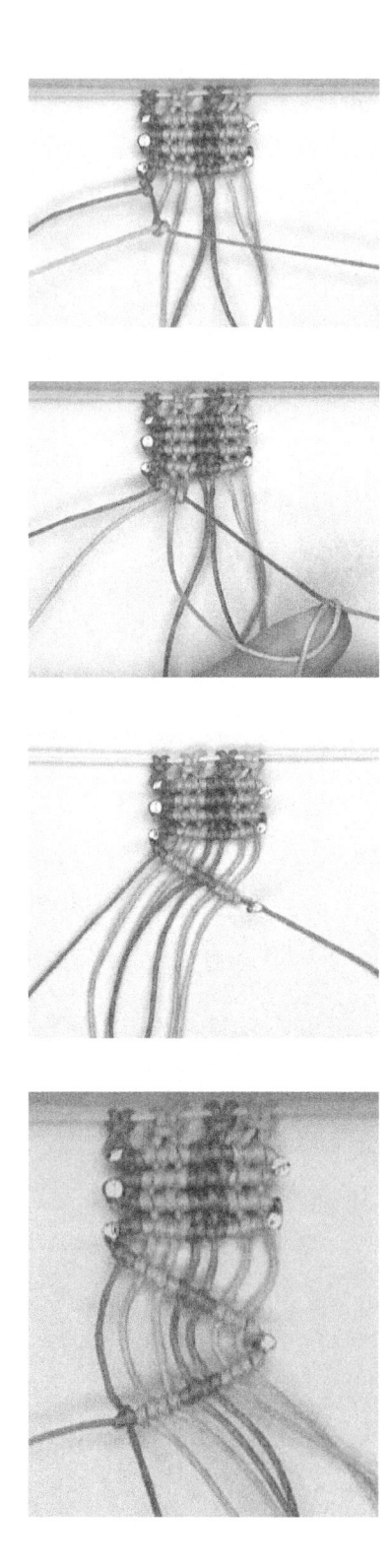

This is the ideal bunch to use for crate hangings, adornments, or any undertakings that will expect you to put weight on the venture. Utilize a heavier weight rope for this, which you can discover at create stores or on the web. Try not to surge, and ensure you have even pressure all through. Careful discipline brings about promising results, yet with the delineations to help you, you will discover it isn't hard at all to make.

Start at the highest point of the task and work your direction toward the base. Keep it even as you work your direction all through the piece. Tie the bunches at 4-inch stretches, working your direction down the whole thing.

Wind in and out all through, watching the photograph as you can see for the opportune position of the bunches. Once more, it assists with rehearsing with various shadings, so you can perceive what you need to do all through the piece.

For the completed task, ensure that you have every one of your bunches secure and firm all through, and give a valiant effort to ensure it is all even. Recollect that training makes awesome. Ensure everything is even and secure and tie off. Clip off every one of the last details.

Frivolite Knot

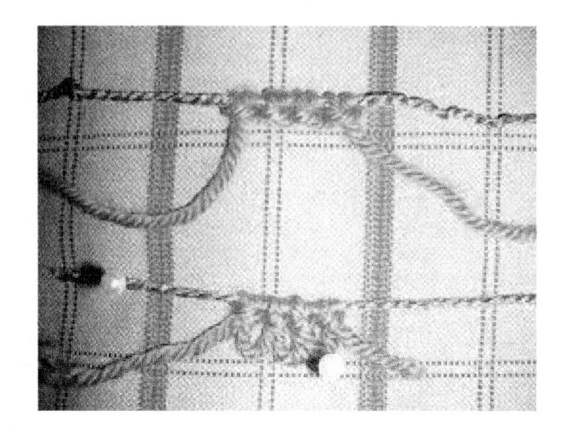

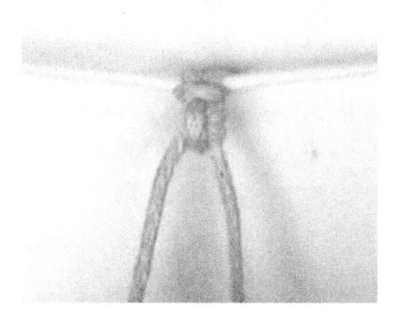

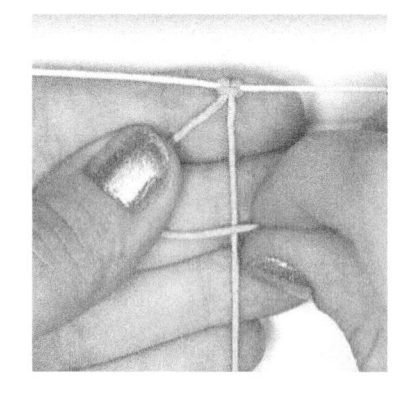

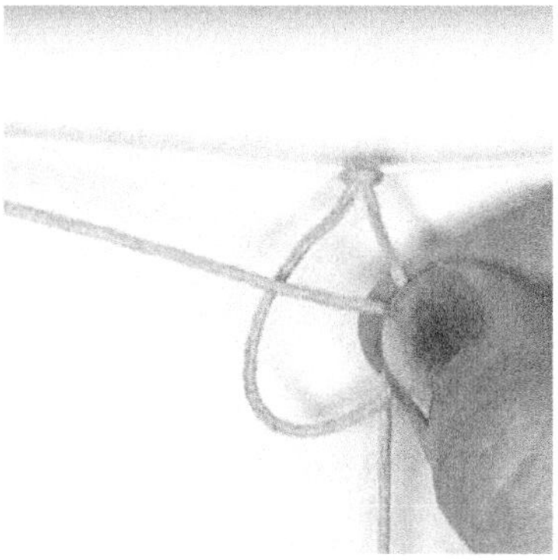

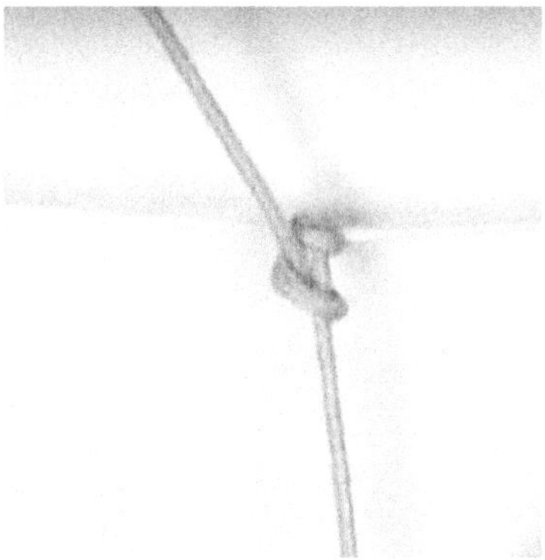

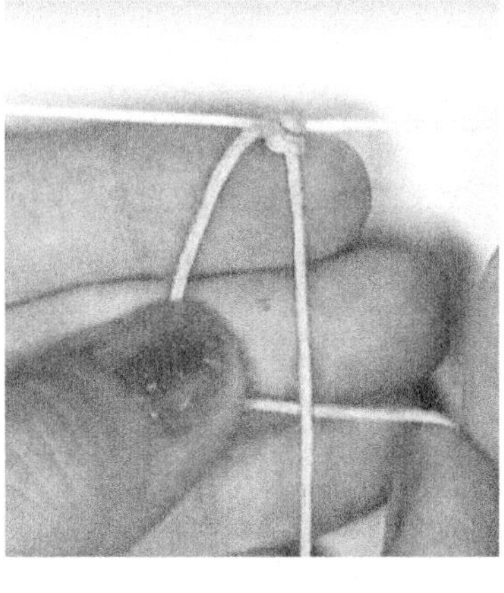

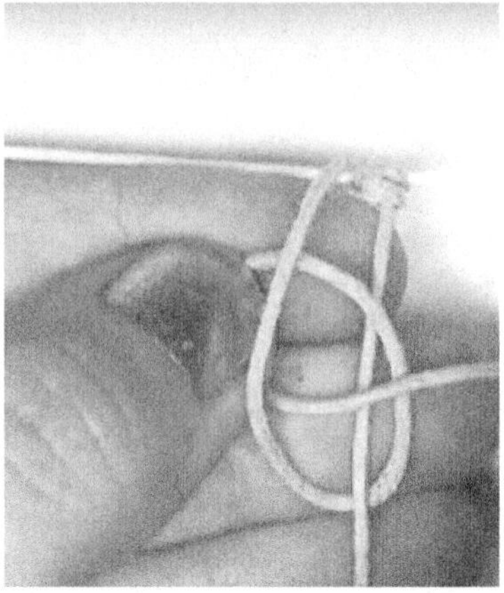

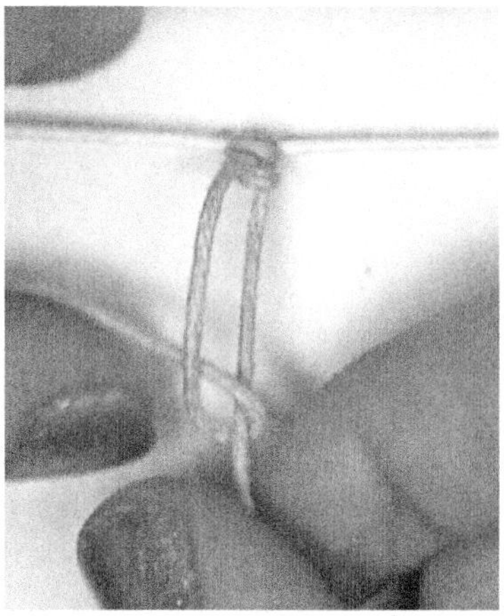

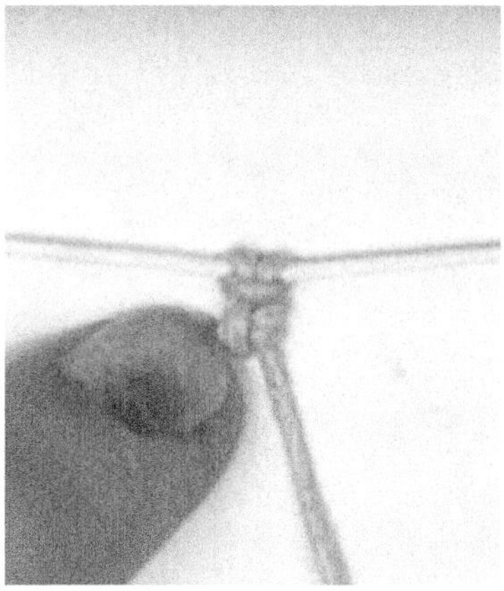

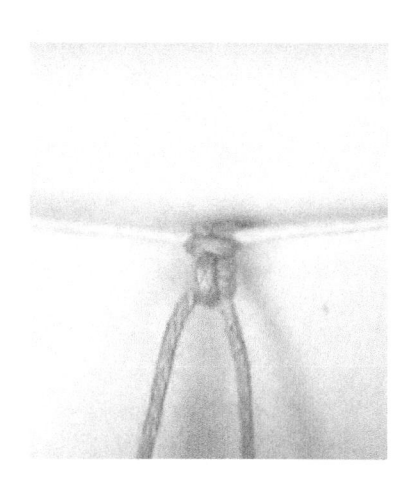

This is an extraordinary starting bunch for any project and can be utilized as the establishment for the foundation of the undertaking. Utilize a lightweight line for this as well. It very well may be bought at make stores or on the web. Try not to surge, and ensure you have even strain all through. With the delineations to help you, you might discover it isn't hard at all to make. Utilize the base string as the manual for hold it set up, then, at that point secure the bunch onto this. This is an extremely clear bunch; take a gander at the photograph and follow the bearings you see. Pull the finish of the rope, up and through the middle. For the completed venture, ensure that you have every one of your bunches secure and firm all through, and give a valiant effort to ensure it is all even. Ensure everything is even and secure and tie off. Cut off every one of the last details.

Flat Double Half-hitch

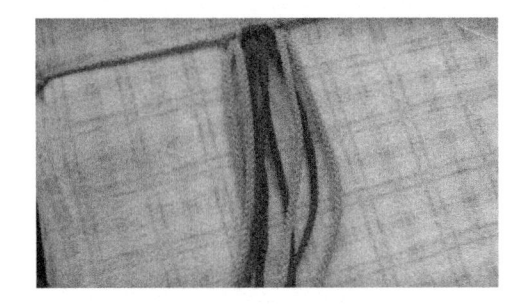

This is an extraordinary starting bunch for any project and can be utilized as the establishment for the foundation of the task. Utilize a lightweight line for this by buying from any place you get your macramé supplies.

Follow the photographs cautiously and take as much time as is needed to ensure you are utilizing the right string at each place of the task.

Try not to surge, and ensure you have even pressure all through. Careful discipline brings about promising results, yet with the outlines to help you, you will discover it isn't hard at all to make.

Start at the highest point of the undertaking and work your direction toward the base. Keep it even as you work your direction all through the piece. Tie the bunches at 4-inch spans, working your direction down the whole thing. For the completed venture, ensure that you have every one of your bunches secure and firm all through, and give a valiant effort to ensure it is all even. Ensure everything is even and secure, and tie and cut off every one of the remaining details.

Josephine Knot

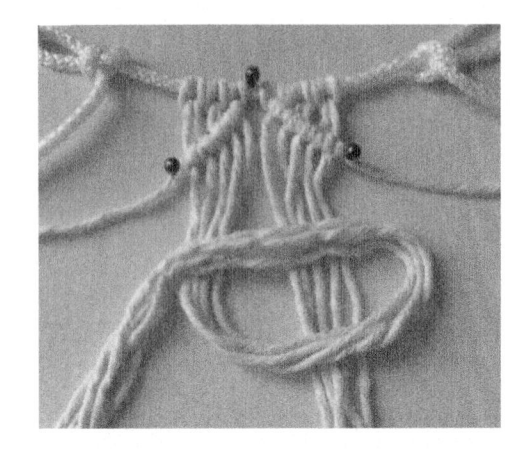

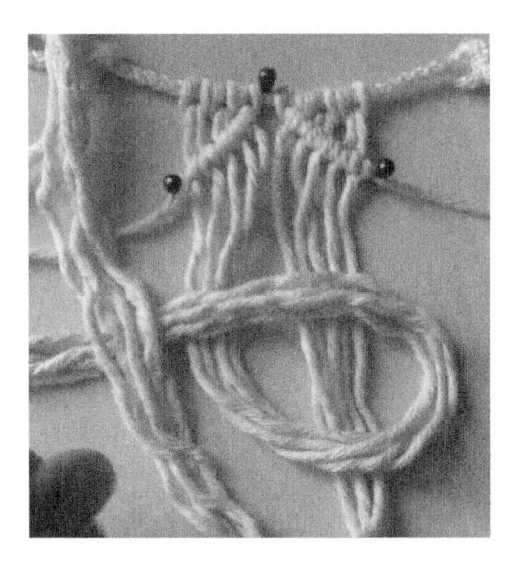

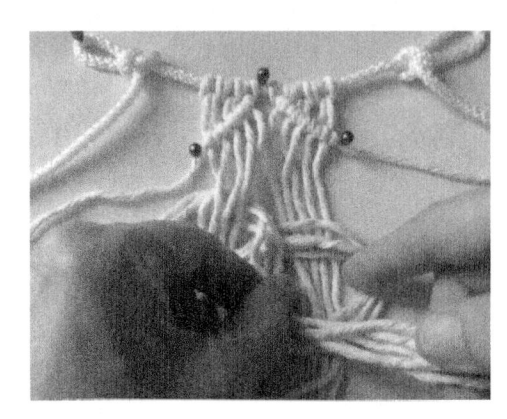

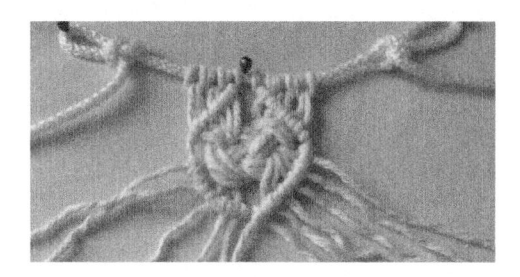

This is the ideal bunch to use for bin hangings, enrichments, or any tasks that will expect you to put weight on the undertaking. Utilize a heavier weight rope for this, which you can discover at create stores or on the web. Follow the photographs cautiously as you move alongside this task. Take as much time as is needed to effectively move the lines. Try not to surge, and ensure the lines have even strain all through. Utilize the pins alongside the bunches that you are tying, and work with bigger regions all the while. This will assist you with keeping the venture set up, as you keep on working all through the piece.

Get the closures of the bunches through the circles and structure the ring at the focal point of the strings.

For the completed venture, ensure that your bunches are secure and firm, ensuring they are on the whole even. It will take practice before you can get it consummately.

Ensure everything is even and secure and tie off. Cut off every one of the last details.

Chapter 5: Macrame Important Tips And Tricks

Picking Materials And Prepping Yourworkspace, Cord Preparation, Finishing Techniques, Begin With Simple Knots

It's the craft of tying rope into alluring or valuable things. There are heaps of different bunches to find that will offer you an alternate look and feel. Like any sort of capacity, macrame takes some time, persistence, and furthermore normally, practice! At the point when you get the hang of focuses, you'll weave up a wide range of astounding and surprisingly insane bits of craftsmanship. Nonetheless, every individual requirements to begin some place, thus, underneath we have acquired 33 fledgling macrame makes that are simple and fun.

1. Macrame Feathers

These slick boho feathers are an extraordinary amateur macrame work for you to appreciate making with buddies! Alluring, wispy macrame feathers have been obstructing my online media locales' feeds lately; be that as it may, I'm not wild about it. They're unquestionably staggering, and I've found myself bookmarking them to purchase later, to hang in the children's region. However, indeed, I was moreover inquisitive to see exactly how they were made. Precisely how on earth do you accomplish that totally delicate periphery?! Indeed, on account of Damaris Kovach's striking instructional exercise, I at last got every one of the appropriate responses. Also, it involves a pet feline brush. That's all anyone needs to know. Honestly however, the potential outcomes are huge here, and I can hardly wait to mess with this technique more. Yet, meanwhile, I trust I'll inspire you to make these at home.

2. Keychains

The best, too as refined present, you can give to a dear companion that they will esteem! Also, an astounding technique for your new macrame abilities!

WHY MAKE DIY MACRAMÉ KEYCHAINS?

In the event that you require a pardon to make a custom keychain, we have you:

- Update the keychain you have had before you can recall

- Develop a cute keyring for the pet sitter

- Offer an assortment of mysteries to a trusted nearby neighbor, so when you lock yourself out you don't need to burglarize your place

- Decorate your backpack

- Embellish your sack

- Develop the snazziest travel gear tag on the baggage claim

- Create an alternate ring for that load of little rewards cards

- Stocking stuffers, birthday presents, present wrap connections

- Leslie made six distinctive custom macramé keychains. You can download and introduce free rules - or on the other hand in case you're OK with essential macramé hitches, we'll give you the basics recorded beneath so you can make do.

The most effective method to MAKE KEYCHAINS WITH SQUARE KNOTS

- Start with keychains # 1 (over frontal area) and furthermore # 6 (recorded beneath right). They're made with a straightforward square bunch - just as its inadequate, anyway extravagant, the 50% square bunch.

- For both, you'll start with 2 50" or two bits of string. Escape clause each through the keyring with a Larkspur Knot, making the external hairs around 2/3 the size of the link. (See the free download for bit by bit pictures.).

- For keychain # 1, make five square bunches, add the dot, make a 50% square bunch underneath it, and furthermore connect the rest off in a tuft.

- For keychain # 6, make around 16 50% square bunches and even completion it with a tuft.

- To give your tuft the best hardened neck, utilize your favored shades of weaving string and consent to the means in our printed bearings or this video cut.

- Separate the line at the closures, trim it up, and you're done!

3. Macrame Garland

I'm feeling significantly better today, my companions. It really was a few days last week too. I'm so thankful for all my mindful cat buddies that remarked and sent me cards and roses. I felt the adoration. On one more note, I remember I said I wouldn't have any macrame instructional exercises, however I can't end up finishing this macrame turmoil. I'm so dependent! While I'm not going to share a huge instructional exercise as I expected, I did as of late completion this fledgling macrame festoon that I accepted was ideal to show to you. It's a little enough errand that you can take it with you. I believe it's similar as weaving.

I've warning that I have a developing number of all-normal just as natural components slipping into our home. I truly don't want it to take over totally, yet I can not acquire adequately. Every normal fiber and furthermore wood is my jam today. It could likewise identify with the truth that it is still late spring and I'm not prepared to give up. Perceiving how I feel all through the wintertime, yet you might remember that my Christmas house trip in 2014 was significantly more provincial than normal also.

Attend A Workshop, Saveyour Left-Over Chord, Study Online

Did you realize it's immediate to figure out some approach to macrame? It basically a couple of key packs to make your complete first macrame experience. Here is the way to begin! At whatever point fall sets in and the days get more restricted, I love to get my record-breaking most esteemed entertainment activity: Macrame. It just took me watching a couple of YouTube records to genius the system, so I'm basically sure you can do it too.

Sort out Some approach to Create Stunning Macrame Decor

Taking everything into account, do you need to figure out some approach to macrame? On the other hand, possibly you're asking yourself, "Is there any way I could figure out some approach to do this?" How hard is it truly?

I'm here to kill the inquiry from this enjoyment retro-creation configuration called macrame. I need to make one thing fathomed before we even beginning. You can do this. I comprehend you may, as of now, have your requests. In any case, that is the clarification I'm here, and that is the clarification I'm forming this macrame instructive exercise. I will address the entirety of your solicitations and, ideally, wipe out any waverings. Right when we're set, you'll a) have a superb, reasonable DIY macrame inside progress or another macrame style for your home, and b) have the choice to add macrame to your synopsis of limits.

Amateur Macrame

Additionally as anything for the duration of regular day to day existence, there is an interminable number of approaches to manage learning another wellness or workmanship. I won't keep up with to be a specialist on macrame. I'm a firm fledgling. Starting with one dear, then onto the accompanying, I am generally going to take you through my trip to give you one approach to manage do it.

I will give all of the assets you need to track down your particular method to understand the satisfaction in regards to macrame. The cool part is that you don't ought to be a specialist to make absolutely incredible expressive subject pieces for your home. Really, it looks fundamentally harder than it is. Along these lines, shouldn't something be said about we get to it.

First: Practice How to Do Macrame

Why might it be a decent idea for you to practice first? Like most anything, this undertaking will cost you a touch. What total? My first 'genuine' experience cost me about $30 for the macrame rope (or macrame string, all things considered now and again called) a few dollars for the wooden dowel.

Additionally, you can't go down to Hobby Lobby or Michael's and purchase the macramé rope or macrame string. You ought to organize it (more on that later). Consequently, in case you're similar to me, and you like to begin a task the day you at last say to yourself, "I need to begin this," I propose to start as I did with a planning experience. I got down to Hobby Lobby and got some cotton string and a little wooden dowel.

Macrame Practice Project

Reasons I suggest a little "practice" experience:

- It includes the time opening while you monitor things for your macrame rope.

- This will allow you to get related with various macrame ties, their names, and how to do them.

- Before the finish of your planning experience, you'll either be remarkably happy and totally restless to go for more basic assignments, or you'll grasp this simply isn't expected for you.

- Finishing this readiness task will give you the conviction to deal with your time and cash to make the accompanying move to your first "credible" macrame experience.

Next: What Macrame Project Should I Make?

Pick what experience you need to make. Glance through photographs of macrame on the web. You can look at Etsy, Pinterest, and Google. Do some investigating to see what's out there. What sorts of macrame tries would I have the alternative to make? Start close to nothing.

- plant holder

- adornments including choker extras or wristbands

- inside beautifications

- bookmark

- keychain

- Greater experiences include:

- tablecloth

- lounger (save an enormous endeavor like this for some other time)

- light foundation

- floor covering

- headboard

- festoon or hitting

Pick the undertaking type. Inside embellishments and plant holders are the two remarkable starter experiences. Where is it will go? This will help figure with trip what size you're needing to make.

Discover a style that interests you. Considerably more freestyle and normal or symmetric with clean lines and advantageously depicted models?

Where Do I Find Macrame Patterns?

Exactly when you have picked what sort of experience and which style calls to you, you're prepared to search for a model. I discovered my model on Etsy for under $5. You don't need to purchase a case. There are a gazillion YouTube accounts that will walk you through the creation of a wide extent of tasks that you may love. Three chief reasons I picked to purchase a model are:

I was glancing through Etsy to get contemplations for what sort of task I expected to make and perceived by then that purchasing rehearses were another alternative. I began to look at a specific work that was actually what I was imagining. Models are a truly reasonable other choice ($5-$10). I participated in the shot at not working one near the following with a video, finishing, and beginning it interminably. Being relentlessly from my PC sounded significantly more slackening dependent upon me.

What Materials Do I Need for Macrame?

Exactly when you have your undertaking/plan, you will acknowledge how much rope to purchase. I comprehended I expected to utilize normal cotton rope. In any case, you can allow your own taste and style to control you as you pick your disguising and material. They sell connection (or line) on Etsy. In any case, it wasn't open in the total or worth I required. After a great deal of looking, here is the affiliation I utilized.

To give you an idea, my macrame experience required 220 feet of 1/4" (6 mm) 3 strand cotton rope. Here is the huge number of materials you will require:

Cotton macrame line (rope)

Wood or metal dowel, or undefined tree member or garbage (for an obviously typical brand name look), in case you're doing divider craftsmanship

- Hanging ring if making a plant holder

- Scissors

- Measuring tape

- Tape (I used painters tape which was everything with the exception of difficult to clear, now veiling tape would also be astounding)

On the likelihood that you would prefer not to utilize tape, you could "seal" the wraps up by gathering the terminations with a get fire moving as another alternative.

What proportion of Time Did my Large Macrame Project Take?

This relies on the undertaking that you pick; regardless, for mine, the veritable work took around two hours.

Would I have the alternative to Do This?

Without a doubt, I'm here to uncover to you that you can.

Have Fun, Macramé Supplies, Difference Between A String, Rope, And Rope Tools Required For Macramé

Pick Design

Right off the bat, pick the spot in house where you hang your new specialty. Then, at that point pick plan with the assistance of web or web-based media. Before, macramé was utilized for making home things like window ornaments, beds, inside decorations, plants hangings and so on It is a phenomenal model that how macramé was utilized around then. Assuming you need tapestries then, at that point rings are fundamental. The way of weaving is a way for householders to make another exceptional and exquisite thing itself. Today, there are a large number of plans and thoughts which is precisely coordinating with the spot which you pick. Make the chart on the page of your exact idea. Use rings, chimes, classical things. For instance: elephants, sparrows, peacock, ringers and diverse different things.

Practice Knots and Start Making Using Required Material

Macramé is a bunch of the bigger universe of bunches, and it's a decent spot to begin with knotting,because with three or four bunches, you can make something that looks astonishing in your home," Before beginning, remind the bunches and attempt it. In the event that you effectively remind, take a stab at rope. In the event that you are fulfilled, begin making utilizing the necessary material like needle. Scissor, yarn, jute, rings and so forth

Together totally required material then, at that point begin weaving macramé. It is a particularly wonderful and creative art at any point have. In consistently and each culture, it is extraordinary art. Materials were utilized to make exquisite improving covers for camels and ponies. Elderly person weave macramé for enhancing their home to look excellent. Numerous things were woven by utilizing this material, for example, inside decorations, plants cover, place settings, shopping packs and so forth Macramé become something one should wear. Macramé is an art; one could utilize it to communicate remarkable style with high quality attire and stylistic layout. Today macramé is bit more valuable than past. New and normal material is discreetly bit significant than past. A clear divider looks astonishing with hanging macramé create. Plants look more appealing and wonderful in macramé inside decoration covers.

Macramé is looking more refine regular and creative this time.

Basic macramé wall decorations can prepare your home. Planner's plan basic tapestries macramé to prep the photos and crowd pay heed. Cowhide and texture belts are likewise made by utilizing macramé methods. More different things are likewise made by utilizing the procedures like arm bands. Anybody can made an ever increasing number of things by utilizing methods. Each method is minimal unique in relation to other one. Material to make everything is same just a few bunches are unique.

Utilizing Accessories

It is ordinarily said that it was acquainted by mariners of Columbus with the western half of the globe. It is for the most part in mathematical example. It is generally utilized in different nations for making items like totes, belts, satchels and some little enhancing things. It isn't just utilized for little items yet additionally for making inside decorations in which the spaces of line incorporate the utilization of macramé is an inventive specialty. In this manner, it is utilized for making extras. The best strategy to reconsider any craftsmanship is to transform it with various styles and consolidate it with various methods and subsequently dresses from macramé was arranged. For macramé hitching, various kinds of materials are utilized, for example, cotton string, jutes, bands, ribbons,leather, rings, chimes, antique things and so forth The worth of macramé can be high using dots, mirrors, distinctive shaded strings, stones, and so on which offers brilliance to your macramé.

It has numerous conceivable outcomes to reuse the texture as an incredible source. Large numbers of the closet things were viewed as elegant are kept at the rear of storage rooms. These can in any case assist with accomplishing a state of the art style throughout some undefined time frame. Styling and cautious cutting of material into long strips make them appropriate for tying and can create imaginative piece of clothing thoughts. These old fabric stripes can be utilized as a material for making style unsettles bolls, blossoms, and scalps as rousing design. Material waste has been used for macramé work in this examination. In consistently it is utilized, its pattern can never be finish. Consistently has various patterns and methods yet it is just what whose pattern can never be end or finish. By utilizing these straightforward methods, you can make your new macramé. You can utilize rings, chimes, and others for recent fad.

It likewise limits the requirement for new material, lessens contamination, natural harm, and energy utilization. Silk weaving waste was utilized for making macramé with sensitive plans. As of now, material misuse of various sorts has been used to create macramé dresses Here you will discover astonishing inside decoration designs. Investigate, you will simply adore this is on the grounds that you make it with your hands. We likewise add a simple method to begin endeavoring a troublesome plan with straightforward macramé hitches. These macramé bunches will look so stunning on your dividers. This macramé tapestry is not difficult to make and comprehend.

Ladies of any age make it at home. All ladies love to make their own. Its pattern won't ever end. In consistently it is fundamental and valuable.

Straightforward bunches and strategies. It has not many methods and stunts by utilizing them you can make an astounding art for your home. From one side of the planet to the other, ladies make it with bliss, sell it and procure a lot.

Begin Making Macramé

Take a stick and require material beginning weaving ties by utilizing these couple of strategies you can make an astounding specialty that you can't envision. In any case, your macramé is so excellent and imaginative on the grounds that you made it.

Anybody can make this astonishing macramé at home by utilizing these methods and stunts. What's more, your macramé is looking so lovely since you made it. Your specialty is looking so classical, one of a kind imaginative, and rich since you made it with your hands. Macramé is the best specialty for time elapsing.

Chapter 6: Techniques And Suggestions

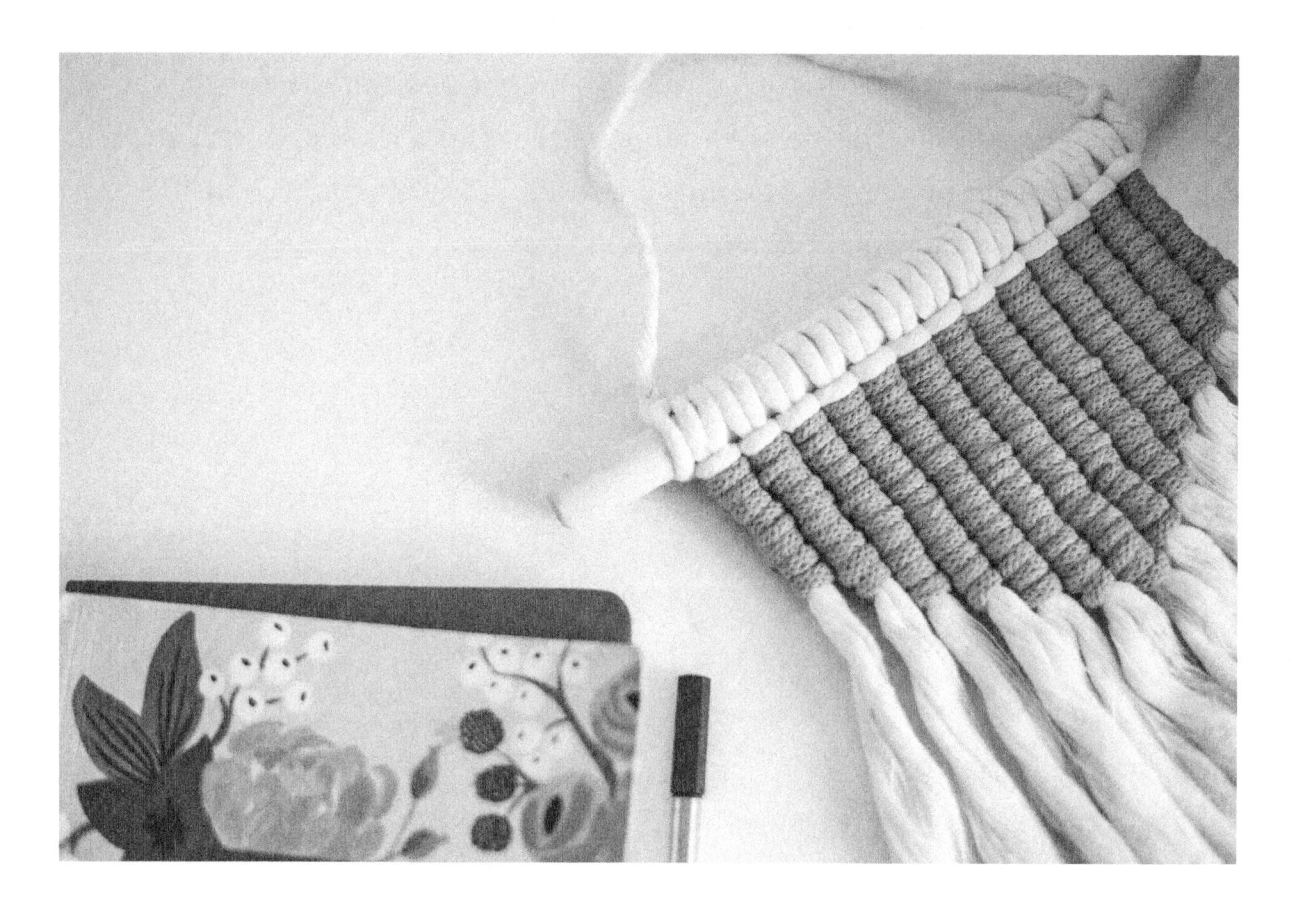

In case you are a beginner or student of the strength of macramé, here are some key tips to help you with avoiding messes up and be completely functional to your greatest advantage. Hitching is the best approach to macramé, yet before you get rolling, here are a couple of clues that will save you time and disappointment when you are essentially starting to learn.

Come out as comfortable with the fundamental bundles with hemp line, as it is everything except hard to work with and easy to fix ties. At the point when you have the principal macramé secures, use nylon cording for your hidden jewels adventures, instead of silk. It's significantly less complex to empty tying bungles. Singing the terminations simply works with nylon cording.

Make a clear endeavor board to use as your functioning domain. It's everything except hard to make and can go wherever, making your endeavor really adaptable.

Persistently twofold watch that the string you plan to use fits through the dab openings (before you start!).

To safeguard the completions from fraying, tie a pack at the completion of the rope. You can use clear nail clean on the pieces of the deals to safeguard them from fraying as well, and this also solidifies the terminations, simplifying it to string those little seed globules. You can in like manner use a "no squabble" liquid found in surface stores to do a comparable movement.

Spare additional pieces of cording to practice new bundles. The way into a cleaned look for your piece is uniform tying. Cautious discipline achieves promising outcomes!

On the off chance that you don't have any T nails to hand, use corsage pins to ensure about your work. In the case of using calfskin cording, make a X with two pins to ensure the line is set up so as not to cut the rope. Recognize the pins on one or the other side of the line crossing in a to one side way, like A X to get the string set up. Recall that every one of these bunches will be the establishment of different tasks that you make, so you need to set aside the effort to get to know every one of them—and practice them until they are what you need them to be. You're not likely going to move them completely immediately—so set aside the effort to ensure you do it just before you continue on to the one.

Relax on the off chance that you don't get it from the get go, it will accompany time, and the additional time you put into it, the better you will turn into. It requires some investment and work to take care of business, however the additional time and exertion you put into it, the better you will be.

Yet, you take a gander at the cost, and you out of nowhere put it down. You couldn't imagine anything better than to have the option to help the craftsman, and you couldn't imagine anything better than to fill your home with a wide range of hand tailored and novel things, yet all things considered, you can't bear to follow through on those sorts of costs. Obviously, it is all great, yet when you can't manage the cost of it, you can't bear the cost of it.

However, you don't leave with practically nothing. You presently have more motivation than you realize how to manage. You need to make and make. You need to do something going to get the attention of your loved ones, and you need to transform it into something astounding. With regards to the universe of hand-made things, you will find that there truly is no limit to the manners in which you can flaunt your inventiveness with the things that you make.

Yet, you have the inventiveness and you don't have a clue how to manage it. You need to make something, however with regards to the genuine execution of the specialty, you feel lost.

What's more, that is the place where this book comes in. In this book, you will discover a wide range of new bunches that you would then be able to use to make whatever it is you need to make. You will find that there is no limit to the manners in which that you can utilize your abilities to make whatever it is you wish.

It very well may be troublesome from the get go, yet the more you put into it, the simpler everything will become until it is only natural to you. I realize you will become hopelessly enamored with every single part of this pastime, and when you realize how to function the bunches, you will need to make them in all the manners you can.

Try not to stress over the tones, and relax on the off chance that you don't hit the nail on the head the first run through. This book will give you all you require to get it going the manner in which you need it to, and it will show you that you truly can have everything with your macramé projects.

Utilizing respectable quality rope

A wide scope of macramé-fitting cotton, acrylic, nylon, and twine ropes with a rope-like contort are accessible in the workmanship and home stores. By and by, I consider utilizing a cotton rope no less than 3 mm in breadth. Cotton garments come in two sorts. Contorted a lot cotton swathe. The plaited cotton snag is woven into one constant rope by (at least six) strings. 3-Strand rope (in some cases called a 3-employ) where the filaments are turned. I saw it in four strands yet it appears to be an ordinary 3-strand string. I love this is on the grounds that working with it is truly simple, unbelievably solid, and hearty, and it unwinds to make a generally excellent periphery at the finishes.

Keep it straightforward

There are such countless various bunches to use in macramé. A solid first-hub is a fundamental hub to know in a square. There are two different ways of making the hub: a rectangular hub, and substitutes a rectangular hub. The entire establishment of most the macramé out there these days is this bunch, and a brilliantly simple bunch for novices to attempt.

Keep your strain even

This one must be rehearsed. The strength with which the bunches are fixed influences the consistency of their size. Practice again and again until you discover a cadence and see your bunches are reliable. You will have to discover a harmony between tying to lose and having your work look disgraceful and hitching excessively close.

Get included and have a great time

The most effortless approach to do something is to get the appropriate assistance. Similar remains constant for learning macramé. Join an individual from the beginner macramé. You will discover answers to your inquiries, will be propelled and will share data. Communicating your creative mind by macramé is probably the most awesome aspect of the journey. Release your creative mind wild and develop something from the heart.

Go to a Workshop

Showing yourself is fun, however we recommend you go to a studio on the off chance that you have any in your space. You get to reach out to such countless similar individuals, and even leave with not just your own personal completed show-stopper yet additionally new companions! We're going on a full US studio visit this mid year, where we will show tapestry, plant holders, cell phones, ceiling fixtures, headpieces, and that's just the beginning! Look at our visit page for a city close to you.

Save Your Left-Over Cord

You should make a few endeavors while you are preparing, and attempt once more. Also, having the right length of simply rope can be your greatest deterrent. You don't need a little string, since it very well may be difficult to add extra to your piece. We likewise suggest that you commit something like 10% a larger number of errors than you might suspect you ought to, as a sanity check. In the new Modern Macramé book, we have an itemized bit by bit factor on the most proficient method to assess the number of ropes you need for your macramé.

That is as a main priority, you could wind up with an additional rope toward the finish of your undertaking! Not to stress over that! We suggest that you save the entirety of your excess strings. You can add the pre-owned line to future ventures, and in the event that you stay tuned, we'll dispatch an extremely unique free example in the following not many weeks, which is a pleasant method to reuse your pieces.

Chapter 7: House And Garden Projects

Jar hanger

This macrame venture is so natural you can make it in only 5 minutes! It's an ideal method to rehearse your first knots!

This is a DIY macrame container holder instructional exercise that you can make with insignificant macrame knots and it just takes around 5 minutes. These look delightful swung from a tree or umbrella for your mid year celebrations.

How about we begin, will we?

Things you'll require:

•Scissors

•Jars (in the event that you avoided ahead, I utilized Yoplait Oui Yogurt Jars)

•Macrame Cording – I utilized this macrame cording and it worked incredible.

•Fairy lights to stuff in the containers when you are finished. I utilized these battery worked pixie lights. (I discover placing a genuine flame in there to be somewhat frightening so be cautious).

Instructional exercise for a DIY Macrame Jar Hanger

Do you have 5 minutes? That is all it will take.

I have carefully written out simple step by step guide that you can learn to be able to make amazing DIY macramé hanger.

The following are the guidelines with pictures

Stage 1: Measure out your cording. You can make this as long or short as you need. Here's the specific equation I utilized which I found on Pinterest some place.

Length of holder x 2 + length of container + 10 inches. I picked 18 creeps for my holder length, so I mentioned the cord twice, at that point included the stature of my container, at that point included another 10 inches and cut my string there.

I saw this length as MORE than enough!

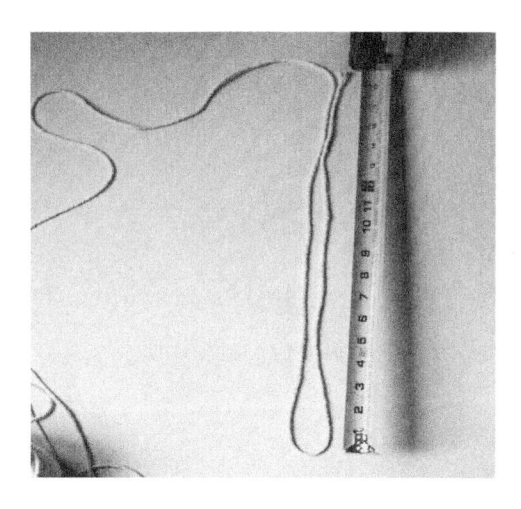

Stage 2: Now that you have your first bit of cording cut, you need to cut three additional pieces precisely the same length. For a sum of four equivalent bits of cording.

Stage 3: Fold the ropes into equal parts. Tie a knot at the head of the overlap. This will be the adorable little holder part. Tidy up the knot by pulling on the strings so it's overall quite slick.

Stage 4: Now hang it up on something – a bureau handle, a door handle and so forth.

Stage 5: Take any two strings and tie a knot a little ways down. Do this with every one until you have something like this. Make the knots even right around.

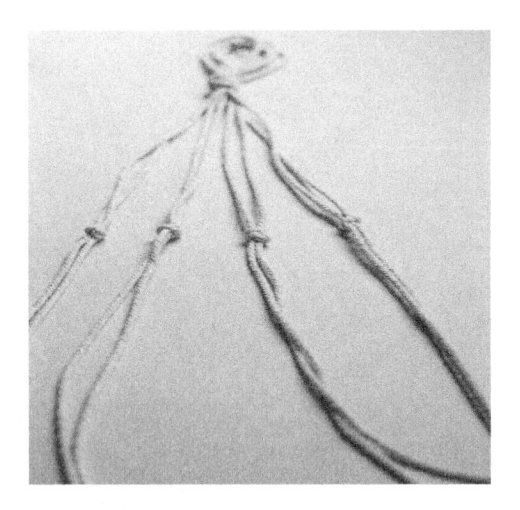

Stage 6: Now.

Go right around until you have four knots. Ensure they are for the most part equivalent. This will be your second line of knots and you will see the holder begin shaping.

This is your light moment!

Stage 7: Repeat stage 6 and make another, third line of knots. With these tiny jars, I saw three lines of knots as the best.

Stage 8: Put your little jar or container in there and ensure it fits. On the off chance that it doesn't, at that point simply alter your knots a piece or stretch them out as much as possible.

In the event that it fits in there – simply tie all the remaining details at the base into a major knot. This enormous knot will be the base of your jar holder.

Stage 9 : You can trim the overabundance swinging from the knot or keep it long. Stuff each container with the pixie lights. Presently hang em' up and appreciate.

You're finished!

Wall hangings

You've most likely observed those great excessive macrame wall decorations. All things considered, everybody needs to begin some place! So here is a straightforward yet beautiful version for you to begin as a starter!

How to build an Elegant Macrame Wall Hanging

– Wooden dowel

– Shirt fabric

Tools needed:

– Texture scissors

Directions:

1. Cut small pieces of texture or fabric around 1 inch by 10 feet. (Tying the texture makes the last venture a lot shorter. Our 10-foot strips made a 3 ½ foot inside wall hanging).

2. Fold a fabric strip into equal parts and slide the circle end under the dowel. String the open closures of the texture through the circle and pull it tight to make sure about over the dowel. Repeat

the process with each portion of fabric, putting them around 1 inch separated until you arrive at the finish of the dowel.

3. Make a line of essential knots, fixing them as near the dowel as you need (We left about an inch between our knot and dowel).

4. Make a column of square knots a couple of crawls underneath your underlying line of fundamental knots (read beneath for bit by bit square knot directions!). At that point directly underneath, include a second line of square knots utilizing a similar fabric strips, making a twofold square knot design pattern.

5. Move some few inches underneath, and include another line of square knots beginning two strips in from the edge. At that point directly underneath, include a third line of square knots utilizing a similar texture strips, making a similar twofold square knot design.

6. Move a couple of inches beneath, and make another row of square knots utilizing the fabric takes from the primary line. At that point directly underneath, include a fourth row of square knots utilizing a similar texture strips, making a similar twofold square knot design.

7. Get it ;)? Make extra row of knots (either twofold square or essential knots) until your plan is finished.

8. Cut the closures of the fabric strips with the goal that they are even. Your most brief strip will decide the length of your wall hangings.

First of all, you have to cut some long pieces of fabric. By long we don't mean a yard, we mean three or four, or possibly five yards. Hold up! Each piece will be collapsed into equal parts and afterward tied, so the length will diminish generously.

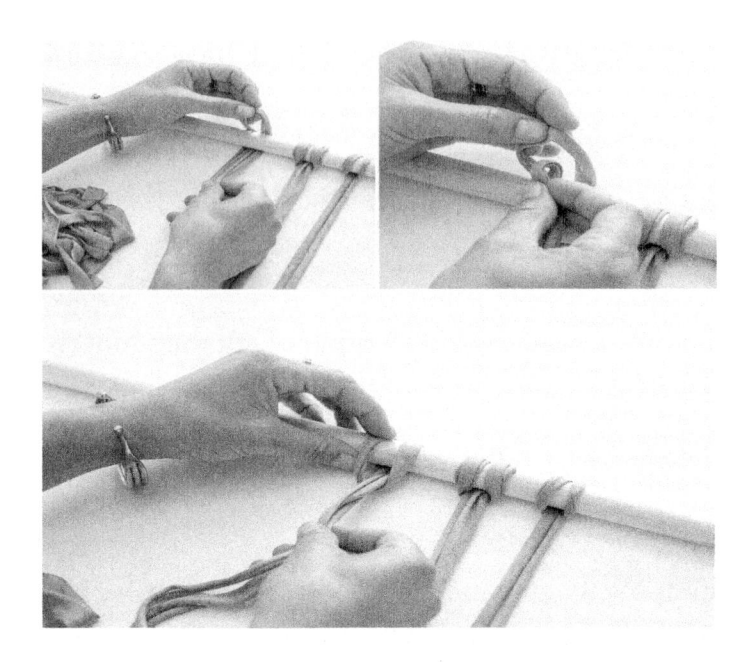

Fold a texture (fabric) strip into equal parts and afterward wrap the circle end around your dowel. Pull the open finishes of the texture strip through the circle and fix to tie down it to the dowel. Replicate this process making use of different strips. This part is somewhat similar to throwing on for every one of you knitters out there. Despite the fact that it's not time to weave, it's an ideal opportunity to hitch. How about we get to it!

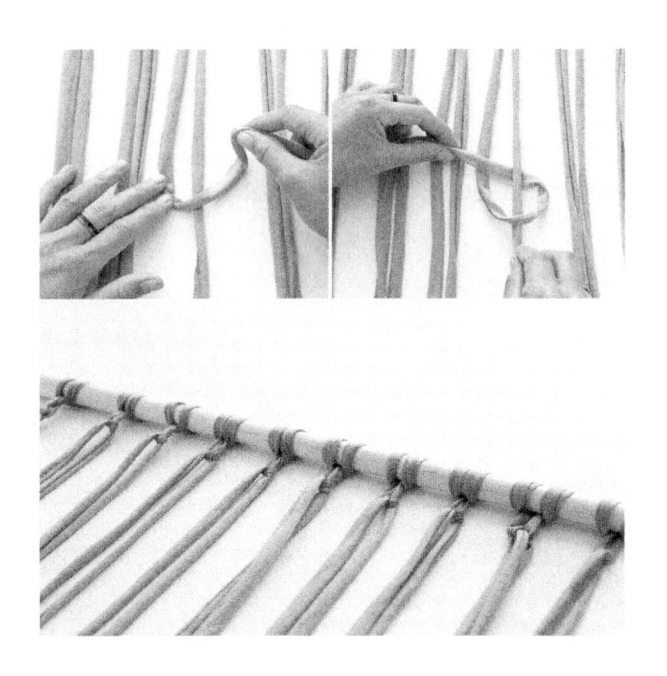

We're going to begin with a fundamental knot. You've done this previously, perhaps even today when you tied your shoes. Make one line of essential knots by folding one strip over the other and getting it through. Fix your knot as near the dowel as you need. You can then leave approximately an inch between the dowel and the knot. Sufficiently simple I guess! The square knot is a far more complex knot to macramé.

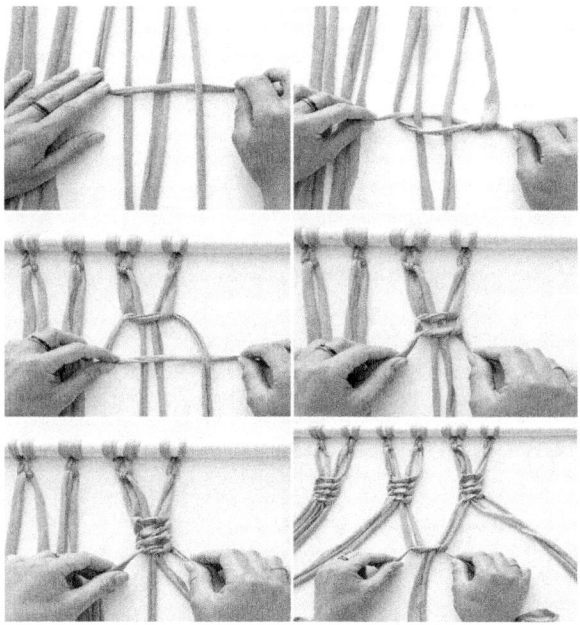

The square knot is a typical macrame knot and it's very basic once you get its hang. You'll have to utilize four pieces of material. We should all beginning on a similar side to make the guidelines simpler, alright? So move to the extreme right half of your venture. Take the four material strips on the extreme right and separate them from the rest. Utilizing the strip on the extreme left (that is the fourth strip in from the correct side of your task) lay it over the center two making a "four." It ought to be opposite to the center two pieces. Weave it under the material strip on the extreme right. At that point, take the strip on the extreme right and get it under the two the center and through the circle on the left. Pull these tight-ish (we left our own a small piece free as should be obvious). Presently make a similar knot again to finish your square. Ta-dah! We bent over our square knots and made a complete row of them.

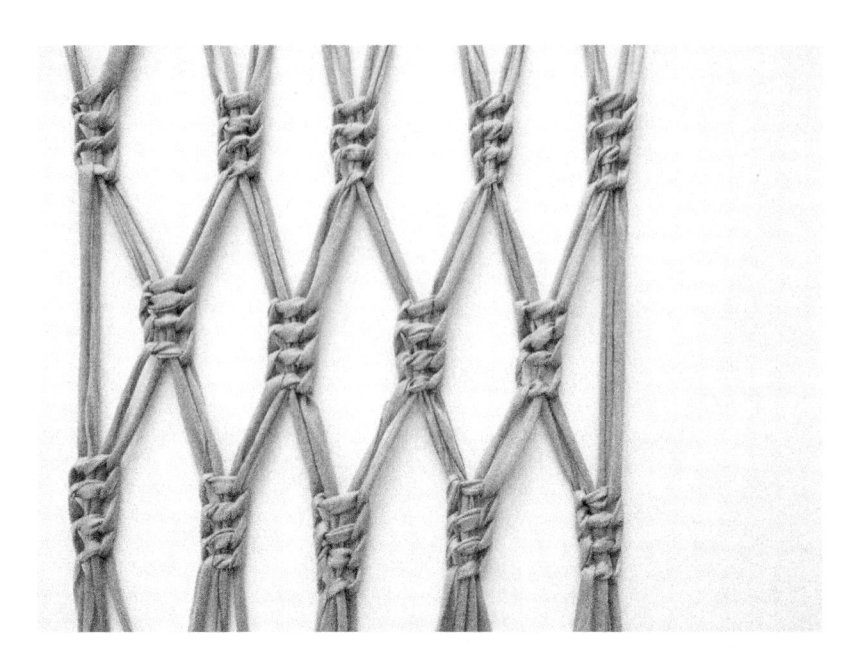

We included a second row of twofold (double) square knots beginning two strips in from the edge to make all the more an example (ohh, precious stones!). At that point, we included a third line of twofold square knots utilizing a similar material strips as the primary column, and to complete, we tied a line of fundamental knots falling corner to corner.

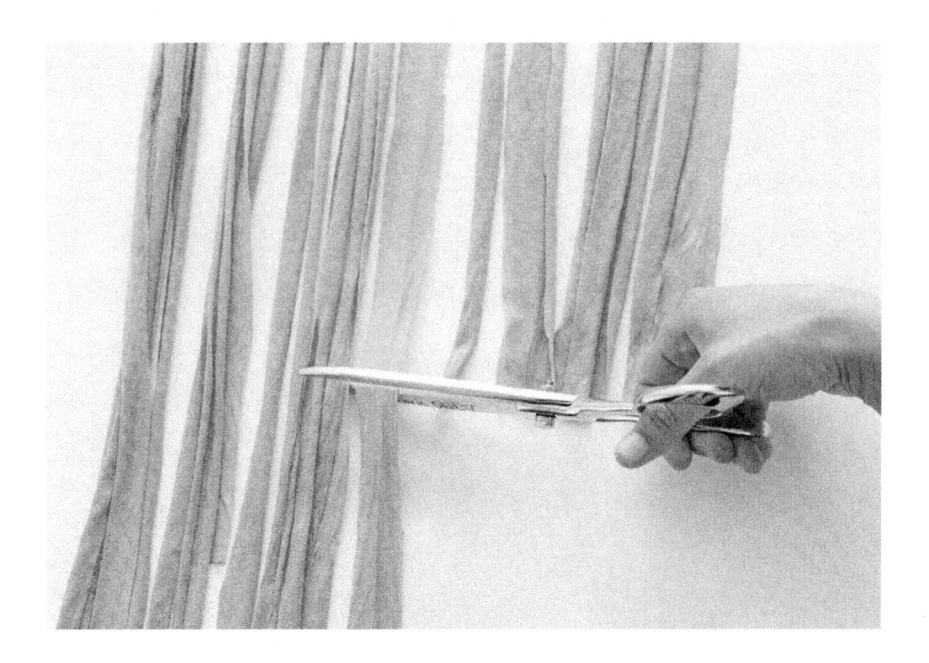

At the point when you complete the process of tying, trim the finishes so you have a decent perfect line at the base of your wall hanging.

Go forward and macra-make yourself another wall hanging! :)

Charming earrings

These DIY hoops are so brand new thus fab I simply should make them! They will look incredible utilizing brilliantly colored strings as well!

Supplies expected to make your own DIY macrame earrings:

•Cotton Cord

•Earring Hooks

•Gold Circle Jewelry Components

•Scissors

•Jewelry Pliers

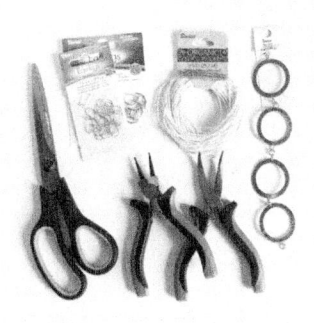

Cut 12 bits of cotton rope around 12-13 crawls long. This measure of string would be adequate for the two earrings.

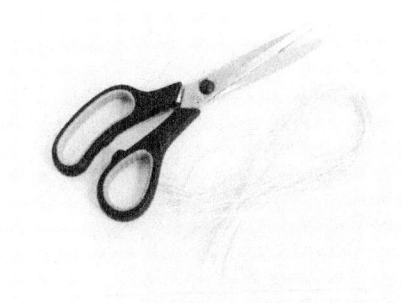

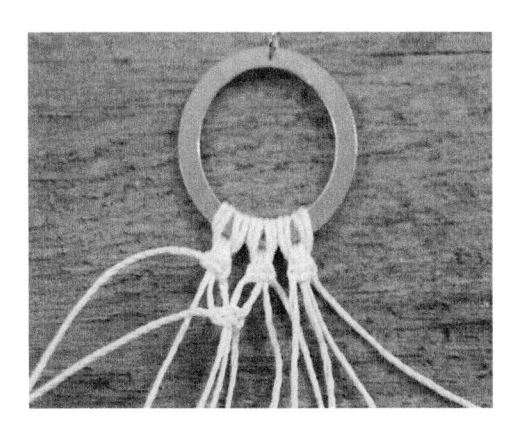

You ought to have 6 strands of string on your circle.

Make a square knot on each arrangement of string. A square knot would go through 4 strings – you should begin with the two external sets and afterward the center arrangement of string so it doesn't befuddle you. You should wind up with three of these square knots.

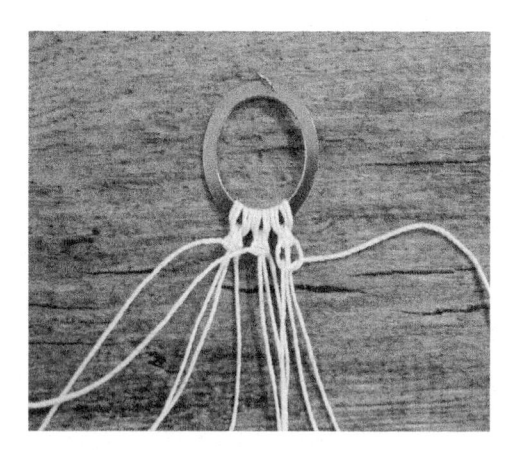

Presently we will make what's called a rotating square knot. Check 2 from the furthest strand, and afterward get the 4 after and make your square knot. You will need to tie it somewhat farther than the upper knots to make some space. Check the following 4 strands and replicate a similar square knot.

For the external two strands, make a twofold half hitch knot and pull it tight, fixing up the subsequent knot with the square knot we made in sync four. Replicate on the other two of strands on the opposite side.

Replicate Steps 4 and 5 until you are content with the length of your macrame dangle. When you are done, remove the extra rope or cord. I like utilizing water to relax the cotton line and agreeable it so they aren't flying all over the place. I likewise utilized a sharp instrument to disentangle the rope to make more volume as appeared on the right earring.

At long last, join the hooks of your earrings, and your DIY macrame earrings are finished!

111

Wasn't excessively simple and friendly for starters? These eventual an ideal evening movement with your lady friends and an ideal straightforward present for any individual who cherishes accessories and boho decorations. I guess you love the macrame trend.

Hexnut bracelet

It's astonishing what you can make with things you have around the house when you turn on your imaginative switch!

Two things I totally love about this venture are:

1) It's very affordable as chips: I previously had string in my locker and the metal hexnuts were 3p each from the hardware store.

2) It's the kind of jewelry I love: I'm not so much into this girly girl stuff.

The arm band or bracelet I made is somewhat unique to the 'twisted hex-nut arm band' and uses macrame rather, which is extraordinary, on the grounds that I guaranteed a few instructional exercises some time back and felt somewhat terrible that I hadn't composed any yet!

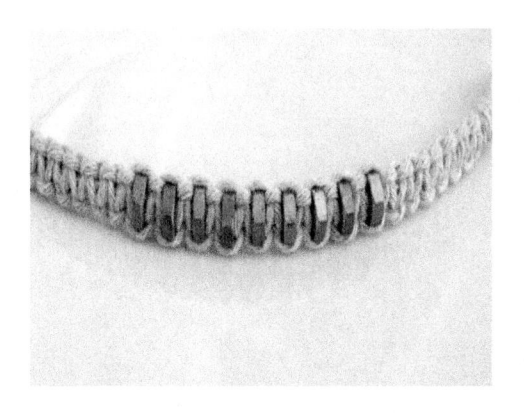

Full guidelines after the bounce! Wish you an exciting knotting!

Square Knot

If it's not too much trouble note: I have utilized distinctive colored cord in the instructional exercise so it's simpler for you to make sense of whats going on!

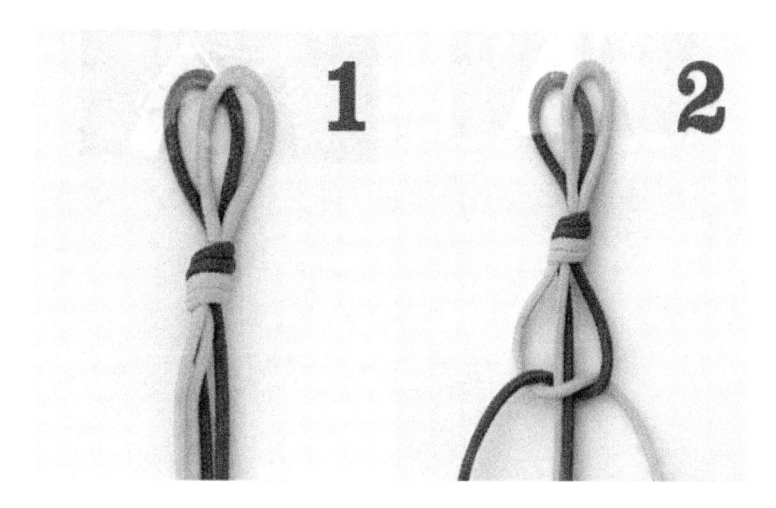

1. Knot four strings or cords together

2. Bring the left string over the two center ropes. At that point bring the correct line over the left rope, under the two center ropes and through the circle framed by the left rope. Pull the right and left rope until the knot fixes.

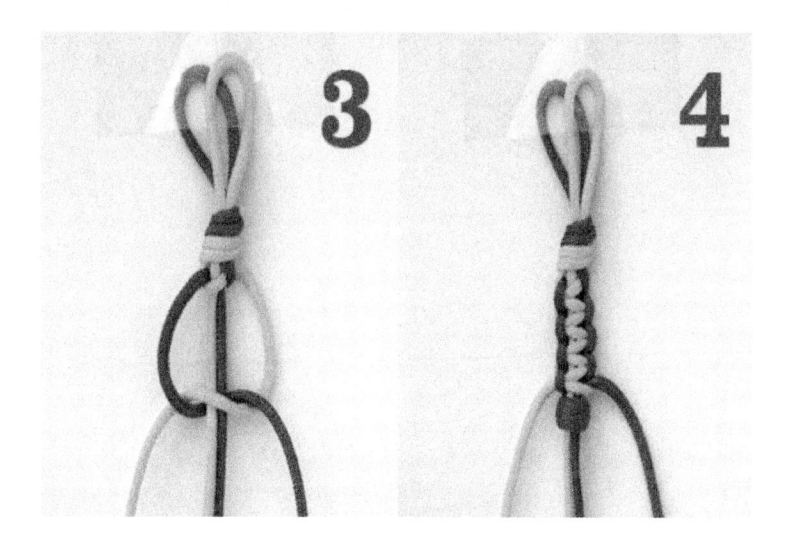

3. Bring the correct string over the two center cords. At that point bring the left string over the right rope, under the two center ropes and through the circle shaped by the correct string. Pull the privilege and left string until the knot fixes. Hooray... you have tied a square knot.

4. On the off chance that you need to present a dab (or hexnut) at that point essentially string it through onto the two center lines at that point carry on tying square knots.

This may appear to be a little precarious a first however I guarantee once you have done it multiple times you'll find it much more easy.!

For the hex-nut arm band I utilized four lengths of string, estimating about 60cm each long and tied the accompanying knots:

8 Square knots

1 hex-nut

1 square knot

1 hex-nut

1 square knot

1 hex-nut

1 square knot

1 hex-nut

1 square knot

1 hex-nut

1 square knot

1 hex-nut

1 square knot

1 hex-nut

1 square knot

1 hex-nut

1 square knot

1 hex-nut

8 square knots

(There's likely a short-hand method of composing this yet shorthand guidelines consistently alarm me so I for the most part give them a wide compartment!)

Chapter 8: Bracelet Projects

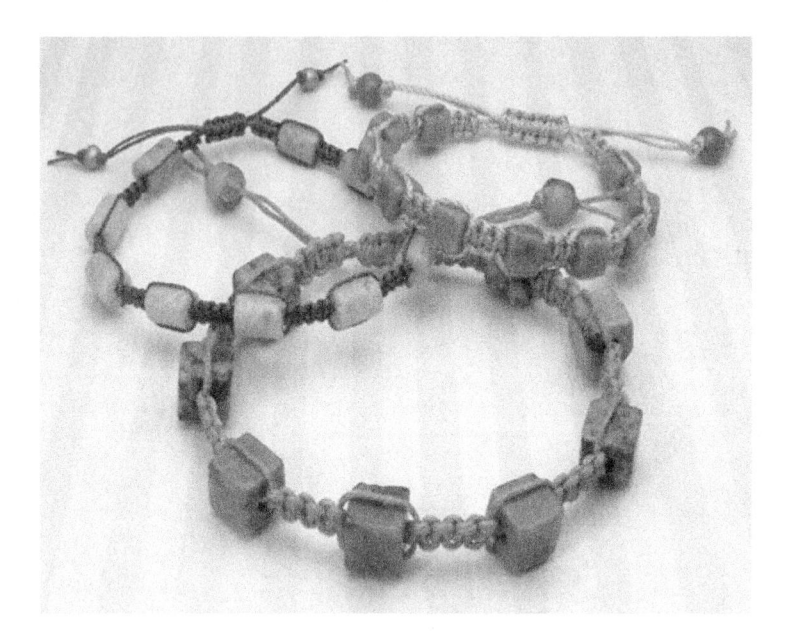

The plan is about the arm bands you can discover in stores where individuals travel, as with hikers. Dabs and wire are effectively gotten, and utilizing these materials, you can plan them to your inclination. The wearer can tweak the length of the lash to guarantee the catch sits where they need it to.

There are various materials out there, regardless of whether it is wires and globules or different materials, that can fill in as long as the dab openings are enormous enough for two links to handily go through! This specific bunch, which is truly straightforward, is found all through the plan. The easier it is to finish up the wristband catch, because of the reality this arm band and all that needed to achieve it will be clarify in this section.

Materials Required In The Project

•Clipboard with a piece of froth center or cardboard decrease to fit as a fiddle

•four yards string I utilized C-Lon Tex 400 for this demo

- Eight or more prominent globules depending on time of wristband

- 2 more modest globules for hangs

- Three right currently sticks

- Scissors

- Needlepoint needle for completing has round ballpoint give up

- Needle nose rings forceps

Prodedure:

Measure out 2 segments of twine, around 24", and integrate them. Then, make an overlay in the texture, embed the twine under, and cut the two finishes under the clipboard about eight" from the 1 stop. The lines could be filler. The filler lines I use are of the shade of lavender.

Stage 1: Cut approximately 2 yards of twine.

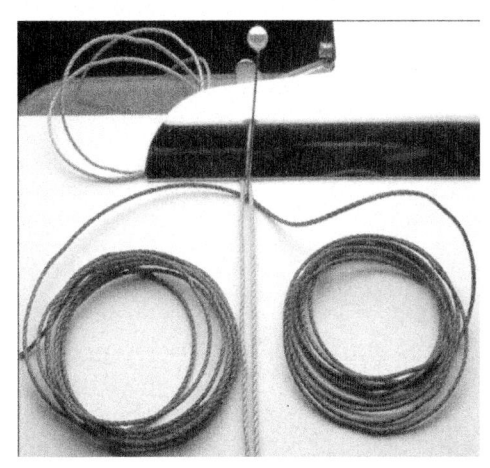

This could ultimately be the strings used to integrate things. In most of cases, I utilize a light earthy colored string for the filler line, and I decide to utilize a darkish shade of blood red for the hitching ropes just for this demo. Pin into froth center board close to the tying twine's middle. At last, we can begin on our strolling rectangular bunches meetings, utilizing the tying lines on top of the filler ropes.

Stage 2: I am roughly 1m (3ft) beyond the mark of the wires, so I as a rule start with the furthest right filler rope. Stick it over the ropes close to the filler dabs, and it will frame a winding on the right. Associate the passed on wire to the flat wire, then, at that point go under every one of the links, then, at that point go up through the circle on the appropriate. Separate the entirety of the lines from their clasp and draw them tight. The subsequent square shape has 66% of the square bunch.

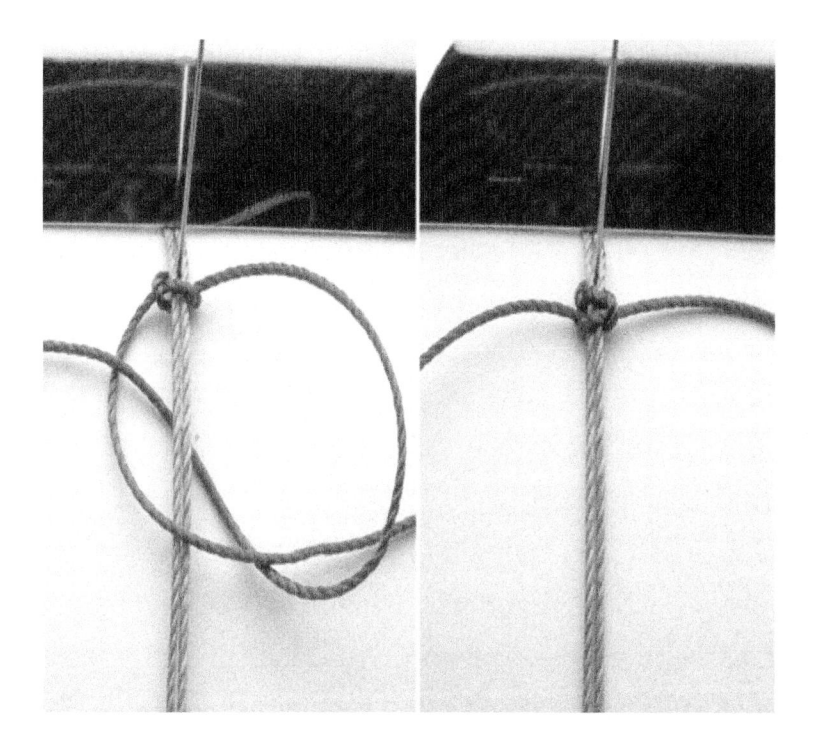

Step to stage 3: Step 2 is rehashed, with the exception of this time the wire is laid across the filler strings at a slight point so a circle is shaped on the left. Start by setting the right string close to the even twine, then, at that point proceed with right down and up through the circle on the left side. Unroll both of the tourniquets, and make them cozy. As should be obvious, you've made a full square bunch.

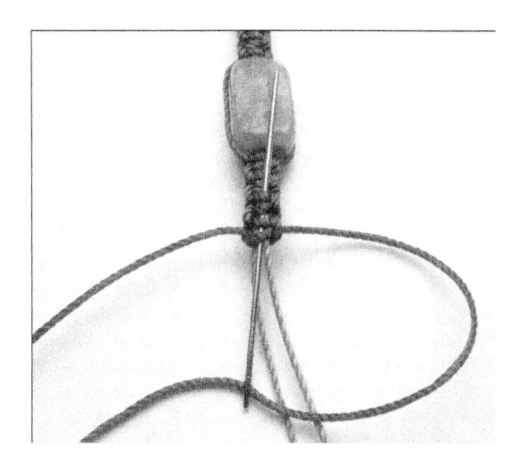

The fourth step is to keep up with the utilization of square bunches and the situation of a globule along the rope in the middle of three to five rectangular bunches. Bunch size is attached to the size of the wire, size of the globules, and the measure of bunches you need. Stretch out this section to the most well-known length. Remember for your computation that the sliding fasten transfers half of."

Whenever you are done, utilize one gems forceps to pull your needle up to the bunch and afterward join up the middle. In the first place, find where your bunches are tight, and afterward you will actually want to line the entire piece with the 3-handle twine. Presently remove the additional length.

Stage 5: The last advance will be to make the fasten. orchestrate your work into a circle and tie it all together by utilizing a piece of wire that is freely twisted around the hitched edges (I utilized orange). Join a pin arm band to froth center board.
Lessening the length of a wire that is 12 inches long. In like manner, as you did in the past advance, pass this twine under every one of the four ropes and tie square shape hitches that are a large portion of an inch long for each of the four lines. The arm band looks precisely the manner in which you likely left it toward the end. Likewise, make a point to avoid setting the needle into the lines which are housed in a catch.

Stage 6: Remove every one of the strings that you won't utilize. The stop of the fasten stage has 2 hanging ropes. Slip bunch and slip hitch arrangement: hold two lines together and structure a slip tie. Then, at that point, place a dot on each rope, and proceed by making a couple of more slip ties. Dispose of the significant part. For everyone you can grasp, swagger your stuff all around.

I'd be glad to answer any inquiries you might have. That would be useful to you. To eliminate one of these more affordable traveler arm bands, and afterward how they finished the closures, I developed this wristband myself. Loosened to craftsmanships charm, support this methodology in your heart's center substance texture.

Chapter 9: Macramé Necklaces

Next up are Macramé necklaces. If you want necklaces that are glamorous but unlike anything you see on the market, you definitely have to try the necklaces featured in this chapter of the book!

Yarn Twisted Necklace

This one is quite simple as you can use any kind of yarn that you want, especially thick or worsted ones to give your projects more flair and to make it modest—but wearable!

What you need:

Yarn in various colors

Water

Glue

Instructions:

Cut two to four pieces of yarn—it's up to you how much you want.

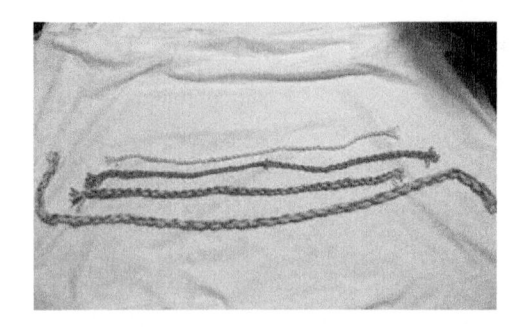

Start braiding, and knot using the square knot. Make sure that you secure the pieces of yarn together.

Knot until your desired length, then secure the piece with a mix of glue and water at the ends.

Leathery Knotted Necklace

A leather necklace has that rustic and earthy feel. Now, if you want to add some edge to an already beautiful thing, you could try Macramé and go and knot the thread!

What you need:

Pliers

Scissors

Chain

Crimp ends

Jumprings

Clasp

7 silver beads

5 meters of leather cord

Instructions:

Cut leather into a meter each and make 4 parts, then make a four-strand braid out of it.

Make use of the square knot to secure the loops. Copy on the left side of the cord.

Add beads after you have done the first two knots. Hold it as you hold the right string. Create an empty knot, loop, and add some beads again.

Secure both ends of the cord using the crimp end. You could also use glue to keep it all the more secure.

Attach a piece of the chain at the end with a jump ring so your necklace could be ready.

Enjoy your new necklace!

Silky Purple Necklace

This silky necklace looks quite regal as it is in the color of purple. With the help of rhinestones, it becomes all the more elegant!

What you need:

Rhinestones

Clasp

2 inches of chain

Thread and needle (in the same color scheme)

6 yards silk rattail cord

Instructions:

Cut string into 6 yards, and the other to be 36 inches. Make sure that you loop the last chain link.

Make use of square knots to tie the outer cord with the inner cord, and make sure to overlap on the left. Bring the string's end right under the center strings. Knot by pulling the right and left ends of the cord.

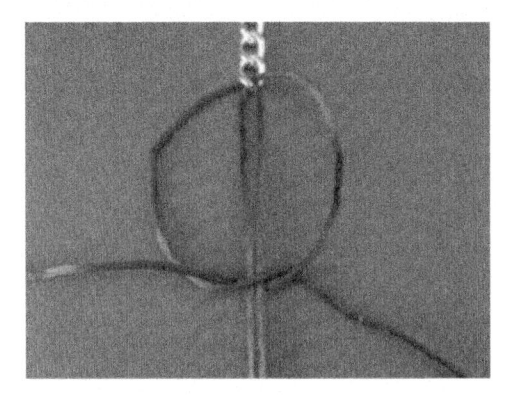

Repeat the process on the opposite side of the chain and make sure to pull tight through the loop and make use of square knots until you reach your desired length.

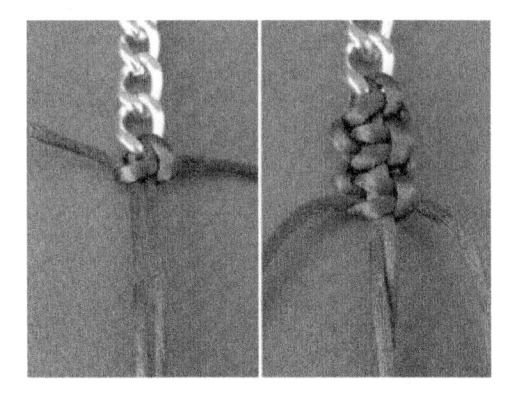

Double knot the cord once you read your desired length so you could lock it up. Make use of fabric glue to secure the ends of the cord together.

Attach rhinestones with glue and let dry before using.

Enjoy your new necklace!

Macramé Gem Necklace

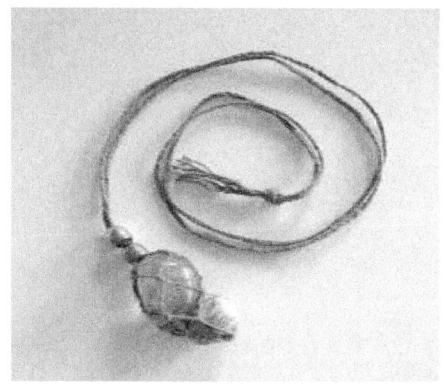

This one has that enchanting, beautiful feel! Aside from knots, it makes use of gemstones that could really spruce up your look! Surely, it's one necklace you'd love to wear over and over again!

What you need:

Your choice of gemstones

Beads

Crocheted or waxed cotton

Water

Glue

Instructions:

Get four equal lengths of cotton—this depends on how long you want the necklace to be.

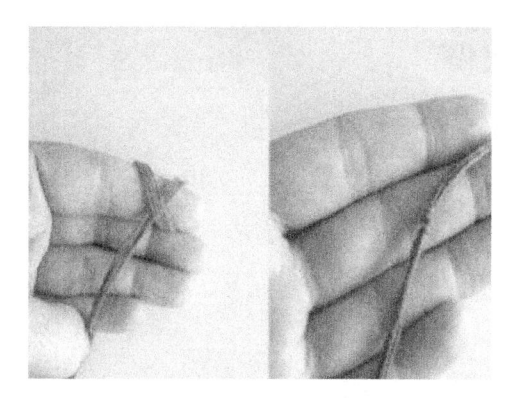

Tie a base knot as you hold the four cotton lengths. Once you do this, you'd notice that you'd have eight pieces of cotton lengths with you. What you should do is separate them into twos, and tie a knot in each of those pairs before you start knotting with the square knot.

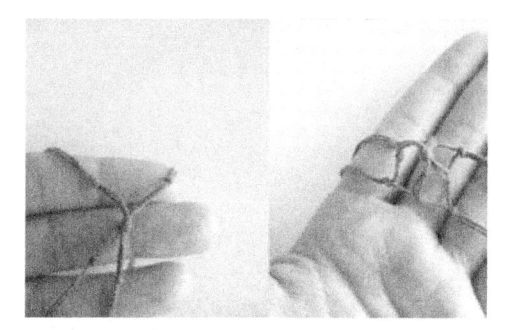

Tie individual strands of the cotton to the length next to it. Make sure you see some depth before stringing any gemstones along, and make sure to knot before and after adding the gemstones to keep them secure.

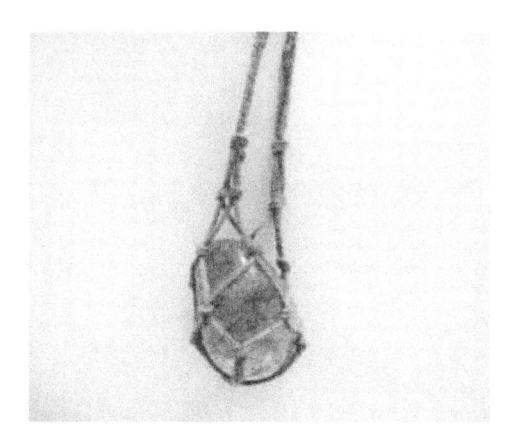

Take four of the strands in your hand and tie a knot on the top side of the bag. Tie strands until you reach the length and look you want.

Knot the ends to avoid spooling, and use water with glue to keep it more secure.

Nautical Rope Necklace

This one is light and easy on the eyes, and is quite edgy—literally and figuratively, without being over the top! It will also remind you of the sea—or the waves of the ocean!

What you need:

Pendant with jump ring or bail

Ruler

Scissors

White nylon cord

Knotting board

Instructions:

Cut 7 feet or 84" of nylon cord.

Then, keep the strands together as a group. Tie an overhand knot around the two strings. Make sure there's 1 to 2" of space between them.

Make an overhand knot 6" away from the end. Tighten the knot by pulling individual strands and make sure to secure it on the knotting board. Separate the strands into two groups.

Take the left part of the cord and cross it under the right corner of the cord. Get the right cord group and cross it over the left side. Tighten as you pull down and knot until you reach 16 inches.

Check the last double chain and make an overhand knot. Tie them 6 inches from what you have created. Add a pendant, if you want, and make sure you knot before and after adding it to keep it secure.

Macramé Tie-Dye Necklace

This one is knotted tightly, which gives it the effect that it's strong—but still really elegant. This is a good project to craft—you'd enjoy the act of making it, and wearing it, as well!

What you need:

1 pack laundry rope

Tulip One-Step Dye

Fabric glue

Candle

Jump rings

Lobster clasp

Instructions:

Tie the rope using crown knots (like what's mentioned in the first chapter of this book).

After tying, place the knotted rope inside the One-Step Dye pack (you could get this in most stores) and let it set and dry overnight.

Upon taking it out, leave it for a few hours and then secure the end of the knot with fabric glue mixed with a bit of water.

Trim the ends off and burn off the ends with wax from candle.

Add jump rings to the end and secure with lobster clasp.

Chapter 10: Macramé Earrings

Macramé Earrings are great because they're definitely not like your usual boring, silver or gold earrings. From neon ones to the more subdued and elegant, you'll surely find the right Macramé Earrings for you! Try these ones, and see for yourself!

Summery Chevron Earrings

This one is something that you could make a lot of as it could serve as friendship earrings for you and the ones you love. It's very summery and really colorful—which makes it total eye candy! You'd surely love making and wearing this one!

What you need:

Ear wires

Small chain

Nylon/yarn (or any cord you want)

Wire

Pliers

Scissors

Hot glue gun

Instructions:

Fold the cord into four, and then tie a base/square knot as you hold the four lengths. Once you do this, you'll notice that you have eight pieces of cotton lengths with you. What you should do is separate them into twos, and tie a knot in each of those pairs before you start knotting with the square knot. It's like you're making a friendship bracelet!

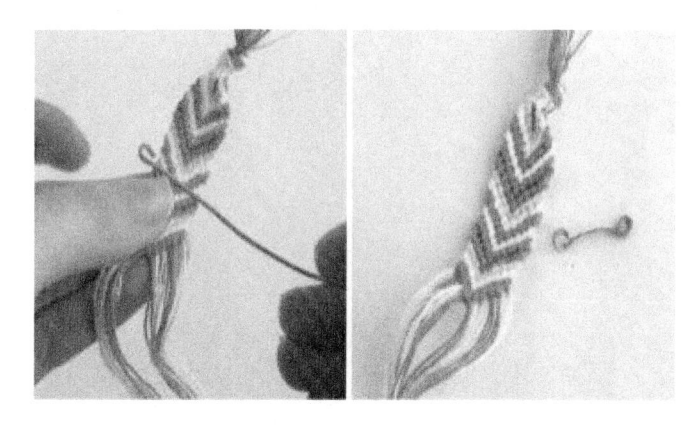

Use the wire to make two loops out of the thread and make sure the center and sides have the same width.

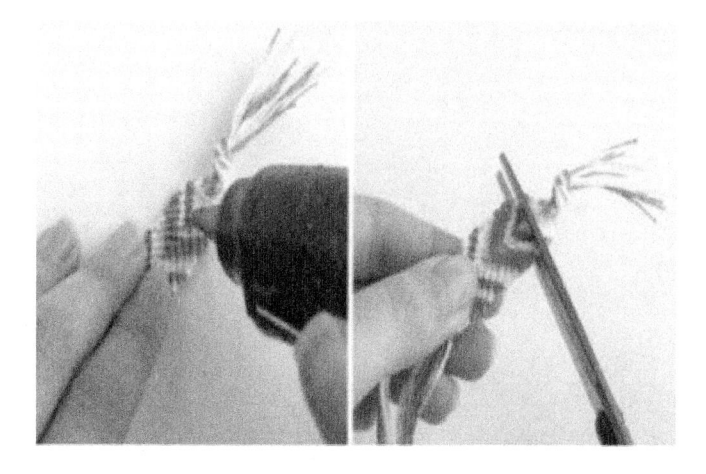

At the back of the bracelet, make use of hot glue to prevent knots from spooling.

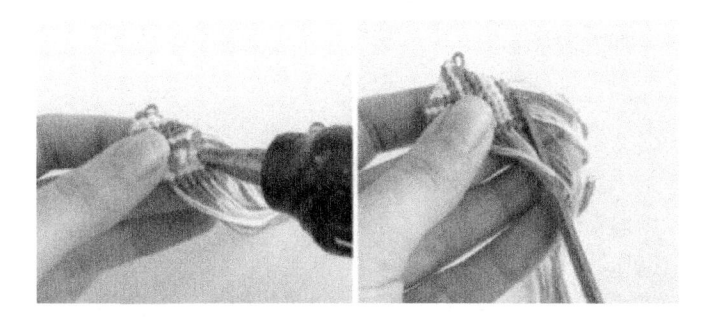

Fold the bracelet around the wire shortly after putting some glue and letting it cool.

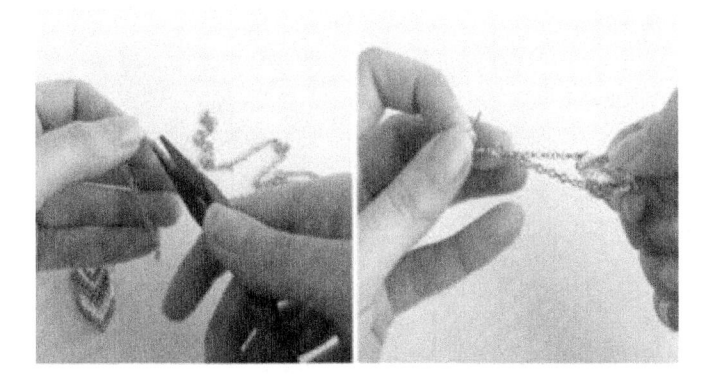

Use hot glue so knots wouldn't come down again. Make sure to cut the excess thread.

Cut the chain to your desired length—or how you want the earrings to look like. Secure the ear wire as you find the middle of the chain.

Macramé Spiral Earrings

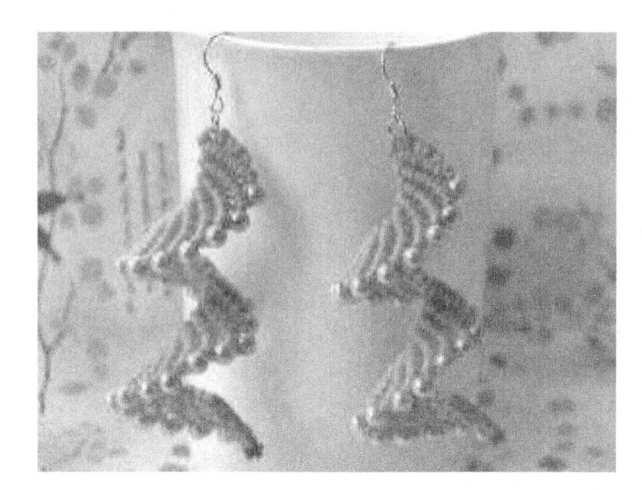

Now, you wouldn't have to imagine seashells by the seashore as you can already wear them—or at least, a Macramé version of them! If this does not remind you of shells, maybe it will remind you of fun parties or spiral stairs. Either way, it's a fun necklace to look at—and to wear, as well!

What you need:

Lighter

Earring hooks

Jump rings

4mm light cyan glass pearl

1 mm nylon thread

Instructions:

Cut three pieces of nylon thread at 100 cm. One of these would be the nylon thread and the rest would both be the working threads. A crown knot should then be tied around the holding thread.

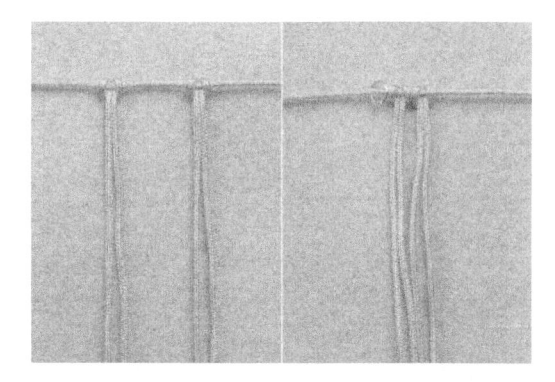

Check the left holding thread and make sure to add a jump ring there.

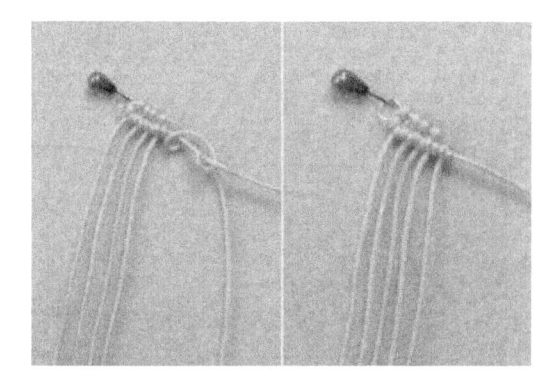

Over the four working threads, go ahead and place the left holding thread there. Use the four working threads to hold the thread and the make a half hitch knot on the remaining thread.

Tie 4 half hitch knots on the leftmost thread and then slide a pearl onto the nylon thread. Secure with a half hitch knot.

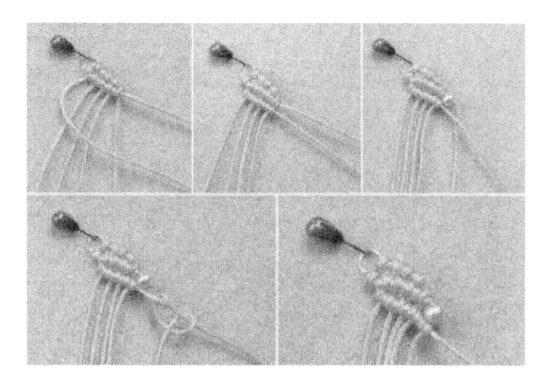

Repeat for 25 times to create a perfect spiral.

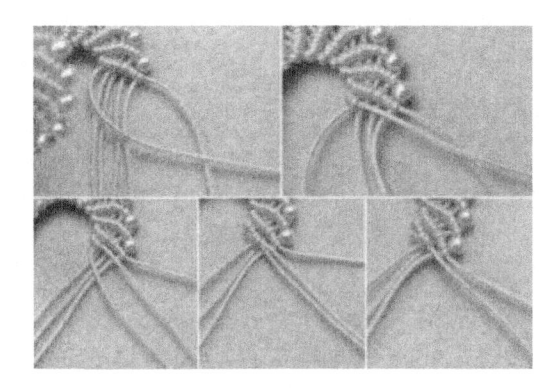

To fasten, get your holding thread again (the leftmost thread, in this case), and let it overlap the thread you are currently holding. Cut one holding thread after tying a half hitch knot.

Tie two more half hitch knots and slide a pearl onto the rightmost thread. Make sure to use the thread in a half hitch again.

To finish, just cut some extra threads off and burn the ends with a lighter. Make sure to attach earring hooks, as well.

Fringe Fun Earrings

These earrings could surely add a lot of fun to your ears! They're perfect reminders of festivals, or fun afternoons drinking cocktails and punch with your favorite people!

What you need:

56" of 4-ply Irish waxed linen cord

2 brass headpins

2 brass ear wires

2 hammered brass 33mm metal rings

22 glass 6mm rounds

Round nose pliers

Chain nose pliers

scissors

Instructions:

Make eye pins out of the headpins by bending the tip and making a loophole, just like what's shown below.

String a glass round to form a single loop and then set aside before cutting in half.

At the end of one cord, make a 3" fold and then go and knot around the brass ring.

Use the long end of the cord to make two half-hitch knots just around the ring.

String a glass bead so that you could form an overhead knot. Trim until you reach 1/8" and the make an overhand knot again. Trim once more to 1/8".

Repeat these steps (with the exception of the first one) and then attach the bead link to the brass ring.

Repeat all the steps to make the second earring.

Day Glow Earrings

What you need:

36" Irish-waxed linen cord

3" 2.5mm crystal chain

2 3" headpins

2 large kidney ear wires

2 12mm beads

Scissors

Cutters

Round nose pliers

Chain nose pliers

Instructions:

Tie an overhand knot by using 18" waxed linen, and make sure to leave 3". Make sure it reaches 1 headpin.

String ceramic on both ends of the cord, then wrap the headpin with a long cord.

Then, tie the ends of the cords together using a square knot, and make sure to wrap the loop.

On top of 1 kidney wire, hold a 1 ½" of crystal chain. Place the rest of the waxed linen under the crystal and let it go criss-cross around the ear wire.

End the loop with a square knot and clean the ends by trimming them.

Put the beaded dangle onto the wire.

As for the second earring, you should String ceramic on both ends of the cord, then wrap the headpin with a long cord. Then, tie the ends of the cords together using a square knot, and make sure to wrap the loop. On top of 1 kidney wire, hold a 1 ½" of crystal chain. Place the rest of the waxed linen under the crystal and let it go criss-cross around the ear wire.

End the loop with a square knot and clean the ends by trimming them, as well.

Hearty Paperclip Earrings

Now this one is really creative because it makes use of various embroidery threads and paper clips to give you earrings unlike any other. If you think paper clips are just basic school supplies, well, think again.

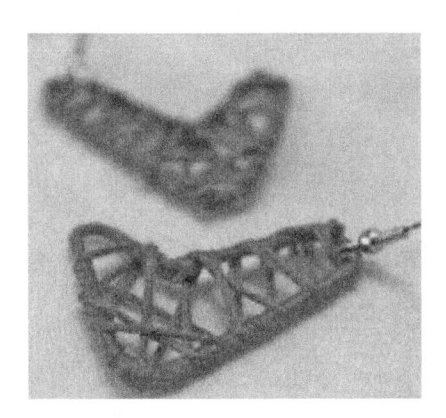

What you need:

Paper clips

Embroidery thread

Earring hooks

Glue

Water

Paint brush

Instructions:

Bend some paper clips until they resemble hearts. Take note that you may have to try a lot of times because it's expected that you may not get the effect right away. Once you have made some hearts, glue the ends to keep them secure.

Wrap embroidery thread just to coat the clips, and then leave some inches of thread hanging so you could make half-hitch knots out of them.

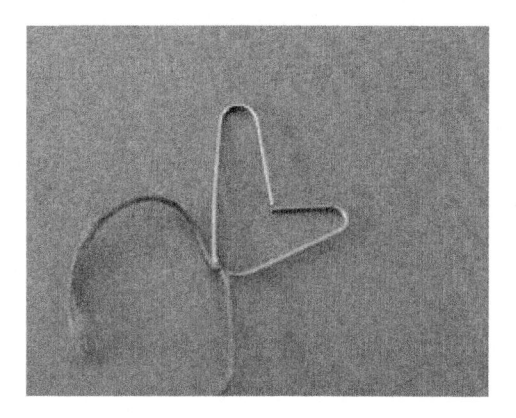

Tie knots until you reach the end and paint with a mix of water and glue to keep secure.

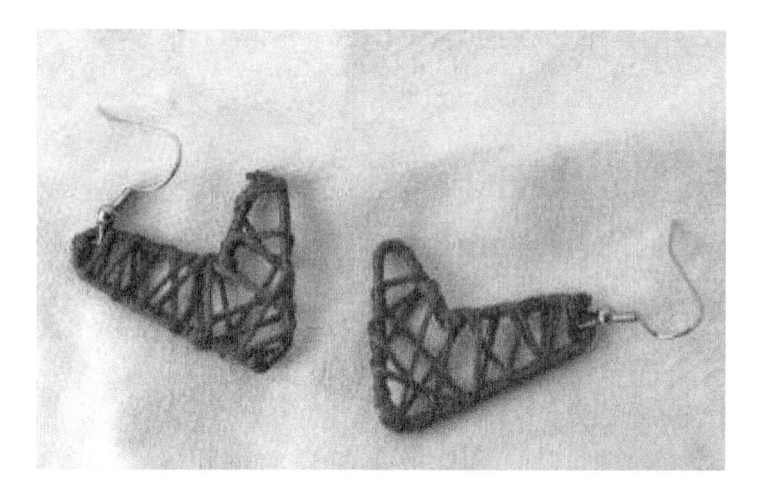

Let dry and then add the earring hooks.

Chapter 11: Other Macramé Jewelry

If you want to make other kinds of jewelry by using Macramé, well, just learn more about them in this chapter!

Sun and Moon Anklet

Anklets add a bit of funk and fun in your style. This anklet will do that and more! It has that ethereal feel as it's made with sun and moon stones—making it all the more magical!

What you need:

16 mm sun/moon reversible bead

2 round 8mm rose silver beads

1mm 18 inch hemp

1 yard hemp (your choice of color)

Instructions:

Gather the strands together by holding them and then tie an overhand knot after leaving an inch of tail.

Anchor the knot by slipping it to the ring. Braid around two inches and then make an overhand knot.

Arrange strands and then tie a 3 inch square knot. Slide the sun/moon bead in the area then make another square knot before adding a rose bead.

Continue with 3 more square knots and then tie an overhand knot. Do at least 2 inches of this.

Go and tie an overhand knot and trim an inch off the ends.

Let the "anklet" slip off the ring.

Enjoy your new anklet!

Macramé Rhinestone Ring

Now, this one is a pretty rhinestone ring that could also serve as a friendship ring. It's quite colorful, but the rhinestone keeps it toned down and elegant. Try it out by following the instructions below!

What you need:

Embroidery floss (in four different colors)

Scissors

Gemstone

Tape

Instructions:

Cut three lengths of each thread and tie all the ends together using an overhand knot. Tape down to secure. If you want to label the threads, you could do that, too, so that you would not get confused (i.e., A, B, C, etc.)

Now, take the bottom left cord and cross it above the top left cord.

take the bottom right cord and cross it above the top right cord.

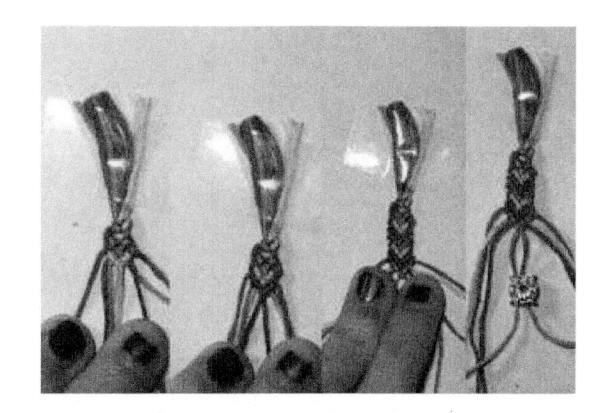

take the upper left cord and cross it above the bottom left cord.

take the upper right cord and cross it above the bottom right cord.

Repeat the process on the other side of the cord, and then insert the rhinestone when you feel like it.

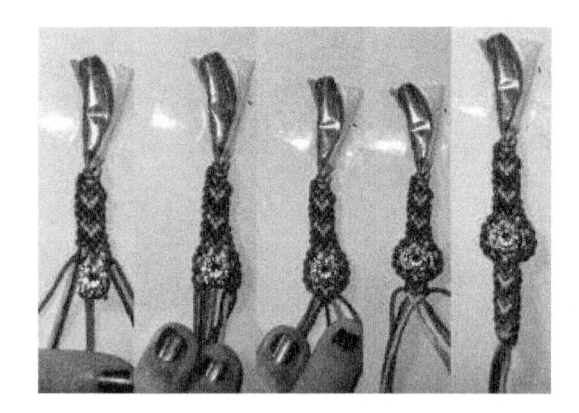

Pull the last parts of the cord tightly so you could keep them together.

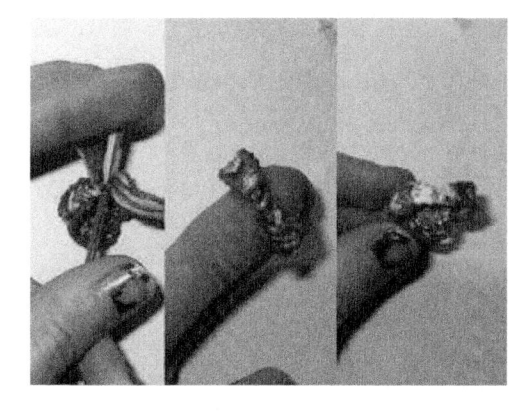

Repeat the process until you reach your desired length and tie ends together. Glue to secure.

Easy Macramé Ring

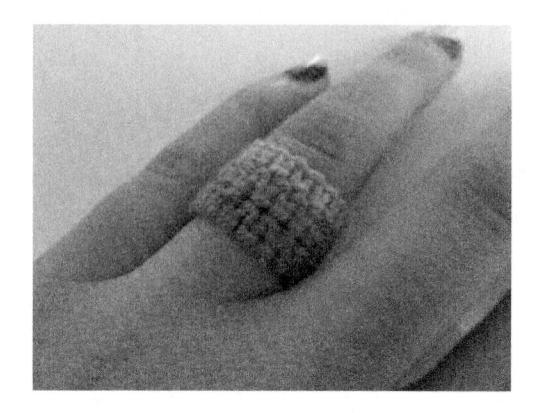

Macramé rings could work as friendship rings—which are perfect giveaways for special events, especially if you're doing them with your friends! It's also not that complicated to make—so make sure that you check this one out!

What you need:

Glue

Scissors

About 1.20 m yarn

Yarn in multiple colors

Round object (just to get the size of your finger with)

Instructions:

Wrap yarn around the round object after folding it in half. Check if it has been divided equally, and then tie the ends with two knots.

Put the right strand over the left strand, and then let left strand go underneath the middle. Keep knotting until you reach your desired length.

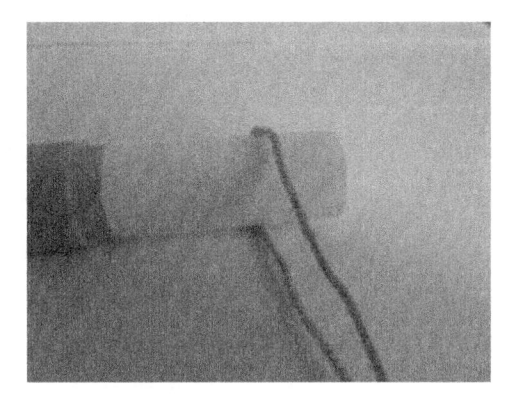

Pull the last knot tightly to keep it secure, and then run some glue over it to make it even more tighter. Let it dry before holding it again.

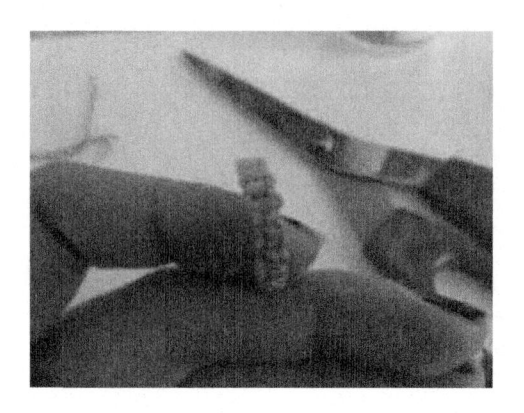

Wear your ring and enjoy!

Macramé Watch Strand

If you're looking for ways to spice up your wristwatch, well, now's your chance! Make use of this Macramé Watch Strand Pattern and you'll get what you want!

What you need:

Jump rings

Closure

2mm Crimp ends (you can choose another size, depending on your preferences)

Embroidery or craft floss

Watch with posts

Instructions:

Choose your types of floss, as well as their colors. Take at least 10 long strands for each side of the watch.

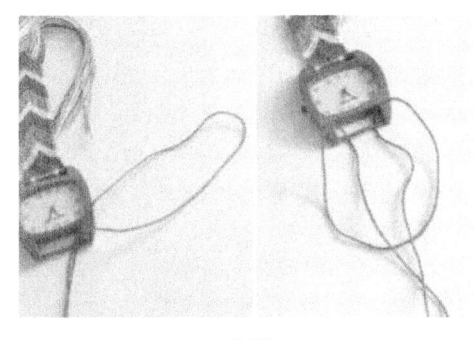

Lash each floss onto the bar/posts of the watch and thread like you would a regular Macramé bracelet or necklace.

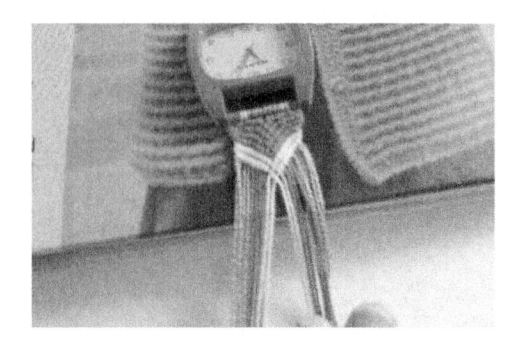

Braid the ends tightly if you want to make it more stylish and cut the ends. Burn with lighter to secure before placing jump rings and closure.

Use and enjoy!

Chapter 12: Terminologies Used

Obviously, you could likewise expect that there are sure terms you would manage while giving Macramé a shot. By knowing these terms, it would be simpler for you to make Macramé projects. You will not struggle, and the making would be a breeze!

For this, you could remember the accompanying!

Alternating

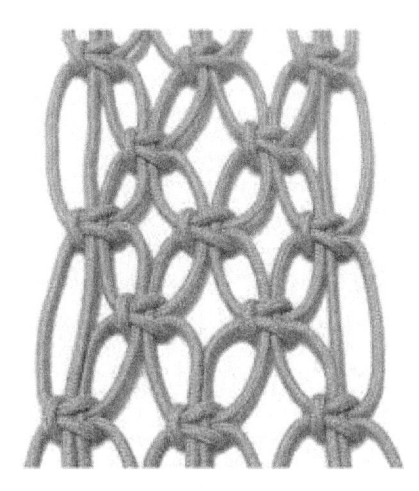

This is applied to designs where more than one string is being integrated. It includes exchanging and circling, actually like the half-hitch.

Adjacent

These are bunches or ropes that rest close to each other.

Alternating Square Knots (ASK)

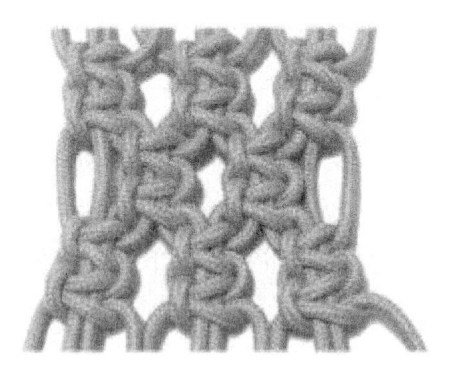

You'll track down this in most Macramé designs. As the name proposes, everything's about square bunches that substitute on a texture.

Bar

At the point when a particular region is brought up in the example, it implies that you have made a "bar". This could either be corner to corner, flat, or vertical.

Bangle

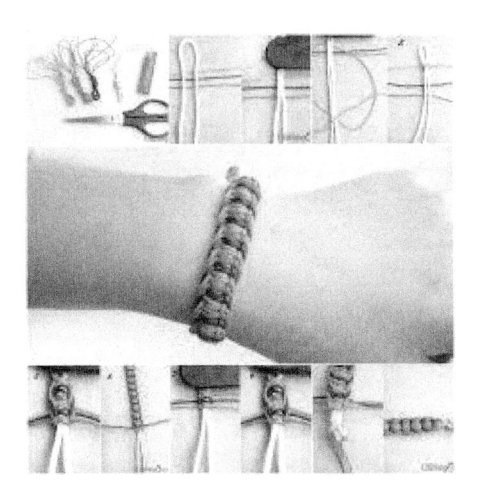

Bangle is the term given to any plan with a ceaseless example.

Band

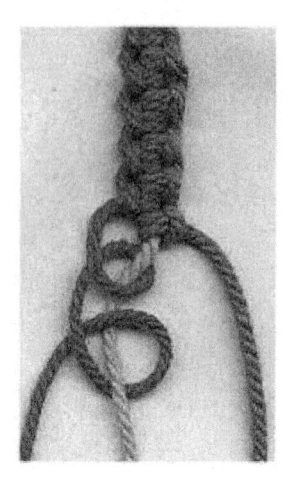

A plan that has been hitched to be level or wide.

Buttonhole (BH)

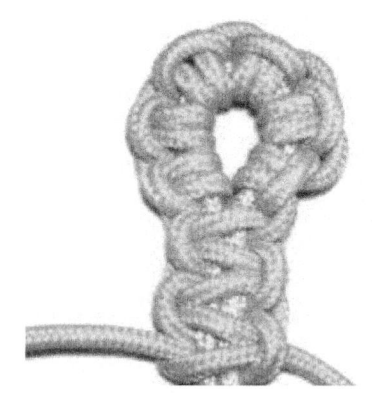

This is another name given to the Crown or Lark's head hitch. It has been utilized since the Victorian Era.

Bundle

This is a bunch that is firm and is in a round shape.

Braided Cord

These are materials with singular filaments that are gathered as one. It is likewise more grounded than most materials since every one of the strands cooperate as one.

Body

This discussions about the principle area.

Bight

This is a part in the string that has painstakingly been collapsed so circles could likewise advance out to the bunches.

Crook

This is fundamentally the piece of the circle that has been bended and is arranged close to the intersection point.

Cord

This term alludes to a gathering of ropes that are running along the focal point of a bunch. They're likewise called "filling lines".

Combination Knot

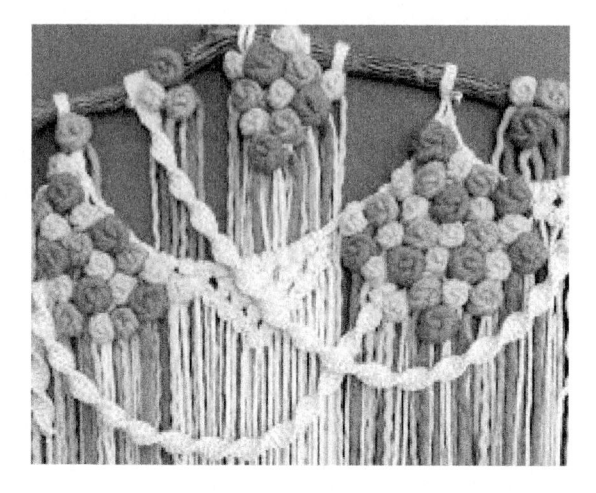

This could either be the material, or rope/string that you are utilizing, or explicit ropes that have been intended to cooperate.

Cloisonne

A dot with metal fibers that is utilized for enriching purposes.

Chinese Crown Knot

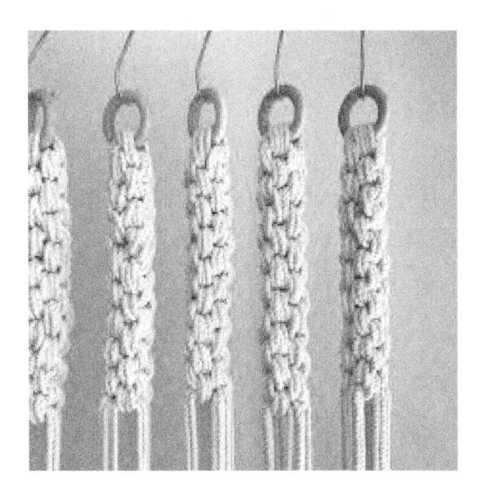

This is generally utilized for Asian-enlivened gems or stylistic layout.

Charm

This is a little dot that is intended to hang and is typically an inch in size.

Doubled

These are designs that have been rehashed in a solitary example.

Double Half Hitch (DHH)

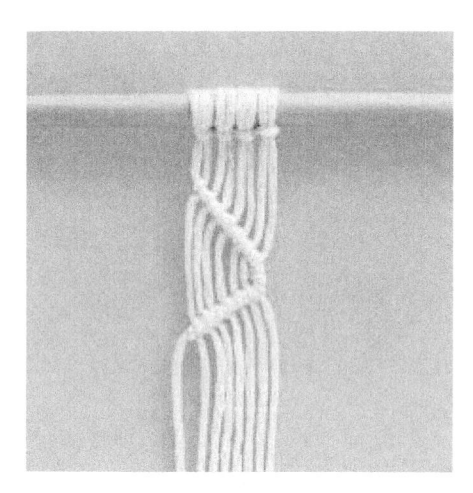

This is a particular sort of bunch that is not utilized in a great deal of specialties, aside from truly enriching, surprising ones. This is made by ensuring that two half hitches are resting adjacent to one another.

Diagonal

This portrays the material's weight, in light of millimeters.

Distance across

This is a column of bunches or string that runs from the upper passed on side to the inverse.

Fusion Knots

This beginnings with a bunch so you could make another plan.

Fringe

This is a strategy that permits lines to hang down with singular strands that disentangle themselves alongside the example.

Flax Linen

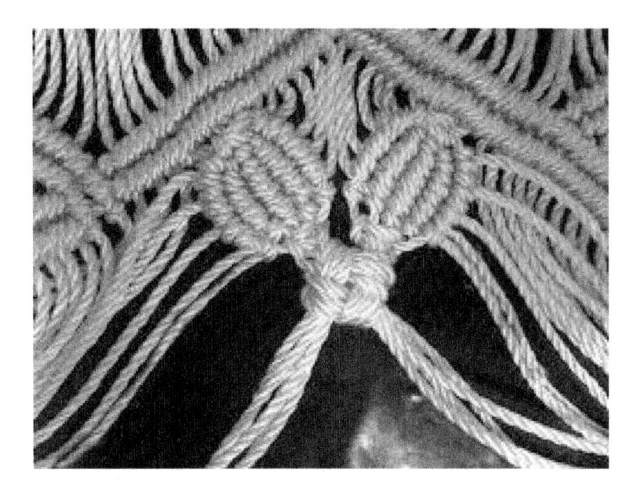

This is material coming from Linseed Oil that is best utilized for making adornments, and even Macramé clothing—it has been utilized for more than 5000 years as of now.

Finishing Knot

This is a sort of bunch that permits explicit bunches to be attached to the lines so they would not disentangle.

Holding Cord

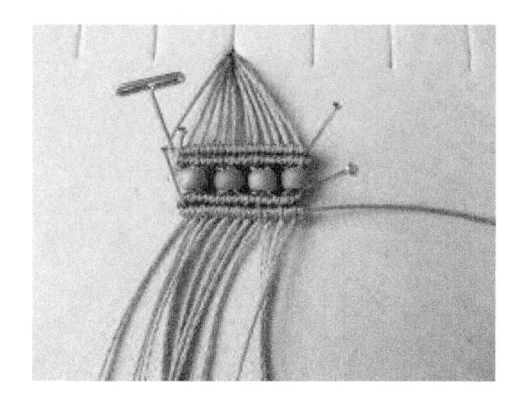

This is the line where the functioning strings are joined to.

Hitch

This is utilized to append lines to ropes, dowels, or rings.

Inverted

This implies that you are dealing with something "topsy turvy".

Interlace

This is an example that could be woven or interlaced, so various regions could be connected together.

Micro-Macramé

This is the term given to Macramé projects that are minuscule.

Metallic

These are materials that take after silver, metal, or gold.

Mount

Mount or Mounting implies that you need to connect a rope to an edge, dowel, or ring and is typically done toward the beginning of an undertaking.

Netting

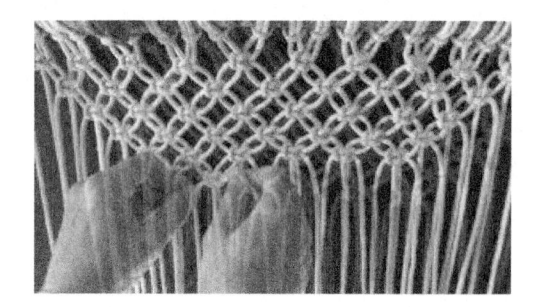

This is a course of hitching that portrays ties shaped between open lines of room and is normally utilized in tapestries, draperies, and loungers.

Organize

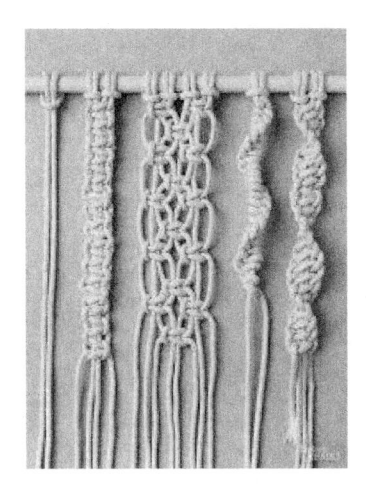

This is another term given to lines that have been gathered or assembled as one.

Picot

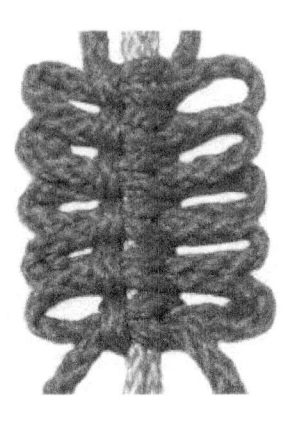

These are circles that go through the edge of what you have hitched.

Pendant

A stylistic theme that you could add to an accessory or choker and could undoubtedly fit through the circles.

Synthetic

This implies that the material you are utilizing is man-made, and not normal.

Symmetry

This implies that the bunches are adjusted.

Standing End

This is the finish of the line that you have gotten so the bunch would be suitably developed.

Texture

This depicts how the line feels like in your grasp.

Tension or Taut

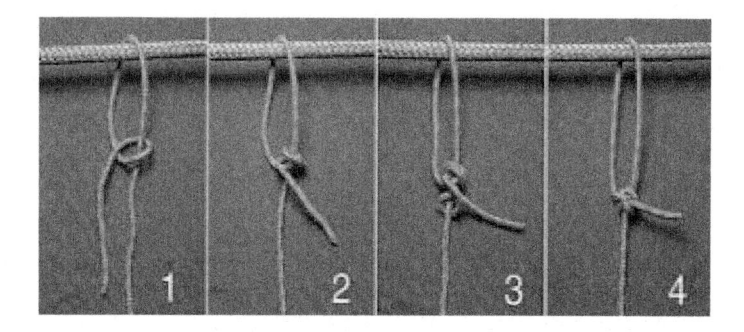

This is the term given to holding lines that have been gotten or pulled straight so they would be more tight than the other working lines.

Vertical

This depicts hitches that have been sewn upwards, or in an upward way.

Working End

This is the piece of the string that is utilized to develop the bunch.

Weave

This is the most common way of allowing the ropes to move as you let them ignore a few fragments in your example.

Tools and Materials

Yarn

The shading part shows a social occasion of skeins that were hued together and thusly have a comparable concealing; skeins from different shading packages, whether or not generally the equivalent in concealing, are commonly uncommon and may convey an observable level stripe when sewn together. In the event that a knitter buys slim yarn of a solitary shading bundle to complete an endeavor, additional skeins of a comparative shading part can, at times, sired from other yarn stores or on the web. Something different, knitters can trade skeins a few lines to help the shading packages blend less difficult.

Metal Wire

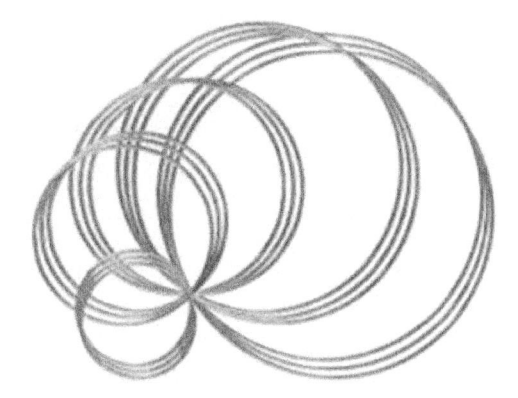

There are diverse business applications for sewing surface made of metal wire by weaving machines. Steel wire of different sizes may be used for electric and appealing security in view of its conductivity. Treated steel may be utilized in a coffee press for its impenetrability to rust. Metal wire can moreover be used as jewels.

Glass/Wax Sewn glass joins sewing, lost-wax tossing, shape-production, and stove tossing. The technique incorporates:

- sewing with wax strands, incorporating the woven wax piece with a glow indulgent obstinate material,

- emptying the wax by relaxing it out, thus making a shape;

- setting the design in a stove where lead valuable stone glass melts into the structure;

- after the way cools, the froth material is removed to uncover the sewed glass piece.

Needles

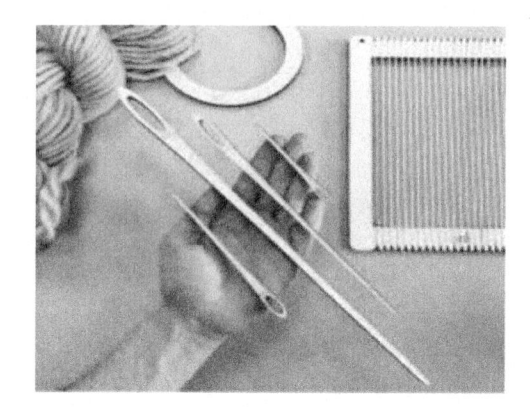

Different materials have grindings and out of the blue handle the yarn; smooth needles, for instance, metallic needles, are useful for fast sewing, while more upsetting needles, for instance, bamboo, offer more disintegration and are this way less slanted to dropping join. The weaving of new lines happens exactly at the diminished completions. Needles with lit tips have been offered to allow knitters to weave in lack of definition.

Tape

Use tape on the finishes of your ropes to hold them back from fraying. I recommend concealing tape since it won't make any imprints on the string. When cutting a rope, you would first be able to put tape on the part where you will cut the line. Cut in the specific portion of the tape so you will have the end and the start of the following line with tape.

Garments rack

To work serenely, it is prescribed to utilize a garments rack. Any kind of garments rack will do, albeit one that is flexible in tallness can be useful. Something almost identical to a garments racks can likewise work: a blind rail or wooden advance stepping stool may work comparably well.

Cord

Cotton is exceptionally delicate and wonderful to work with, while jute, for example, could hurt on your hands while working with it. Shirt yarn is modest and very simple to discover. Yet, you should consider that the vast majority of the T-shirt yarn will in general be a bit versatile, which makes it less reasonable for hanging objects which need to convey some weight like plant holders.

Another angle to consider is whether to pick a plaited or twined string. Interlaced ropes are less inclined to fraying, while the twined rope is a lot simpler to shred.

At last, think about the rope thickness: with a thicker rope, you will actually want to make great, enormous scope pieces, and with a better rope, you can accomplish a shocking complexity in your examples.

Others are:

Filaments

Various scholars and activities will utilize various words to depict hitching material, like strings, ropes, ropes or strands. Once more, this is to forestall the composition and perusing of the task from turning out to be extremely redundant, yet everything implies exactly the same thing: the length of the fiber you're utilizing.

Dynamic and latent

You can discover the terms dynamic and latent string utilized when following macramé projects. Dynamic rope alludes to the strings that are utilized to tie the bunches, and the latent ones are not. Regardless of whether a string is dynamic while making a plan.

Refocusing

Gatherings of two, three or four strings are utilized in numerous macramé projects. Refocusing is a term used to depict the method involved with joining ropes from two nearby gatherings. For instance, if two gatherings of two strings are utilized, the center two ropes will be joined.

Securing

Macramé ties are a lot simpler to tie, particularly toward the start of the piece, in case they are rigid. You can do this by mounting the strings somehow or another. A slip hitch is regularly used to append strings to a strong surface as it is a simple bunch to detach once the task has been finished. Another technique is to utilize pins to get the strings on the hitching board.

Sennit–

Sennit is a length of at least two bunches of a solitary sort. For instance, if an example says you should tie a sennit of five square bunches, it implies you should tie five square bunches in a steady progression. Sennit is now and then spelt as a sinnet, as well.

Hitching sheets

Macramé tying sheets can be purchased or made in various manners. A basic board can be made utilizing a typical clipboard; the strings are gotten under an enormous clasp. Another approach to make a straightforward board is to utilize a stopper notice board and pins. Thick plug tiles could likewise be utilized the same way. Some industrially accessible sheets are set apart with estimations that are a valuable component. In the event that you choose to make your own board, you can without much of a stretch add it utilizing a ruler and an indelible marker.

Utilizing a macramé board makes a spot for securing your lines while working and furthermore makes putting away and moving undertakings simpler. The board can be slipped into a pack and moved without any problem.

Overseeing rope lengths

Macramé projects regularly include the utilization of many long line lengths, which can be tied and snared in one another during activity. To stay away from this, ropes can be packaged up or twisted around themselves and inexactly hitched to make a sensible length. As you work through the undertaking, you can unfasten the bunch and delivery more strings before you retied it. The ropes can likewise be gotten utilizing elastic groups instead of bunches.

Another approach to make long rope lengths more reasonable is to utilize little spools known as bobbins.

They can without much of a stretch be purchased online by the names ' macramé bobbin' or' Kumihimo bobbins.' The strings are folded over them and got, passing on a length to work with. As this length is utilized, more string can without much of a stretch be delivered from the loop.

Chapter 13: Tips And Tricks On How To Make Different Knots For Beginners

Try not to Go Overboard in the Crafting Aisle

It is delightful, correct? Every one of the cushioned chunks of yarn and sparkly needles sparkling before you? Do you imagine yourself sitting serenely, sewing with your delightful needles, and making flawless gifts?

As you meander down the path, delicately ignoring your fingertips the diversely finished fleeces, you picture every one of the lovely artworks you will make for your loved ones. A few hundred dollars later and making room or box spilling over with new toys, it hits you that you do not know what most importantly for sure you need to do. Or then again you start on a task and disdain the manner in which aluminum needles feel in your grasp, yet every time you contact the bamboo needles your companion utilizes, you faint. You have a heap of thoughts you never contact yet are continually running back to the store to snatch only one a greater amount of that one thing you utilize constantly. Save yourself the anguish and bother, get a couple of the nuts and bolts to begin, and afterward add on as you attempt new methods or instruments.

Set aside Your Cash... in the Beginning

The pretty, shimmering, and beautiful yarn is appealing. At the point when it is delicate or has an incredible surface, you simply need to run your hands over it over and over. As you start learning, you will sew and eliminate fastens, making a ton of mileage on the yarn. All the beautiful sparkle and surface will be destroyed. Your yarn will tangle—not a pleasant method to begin your weaving experience. You will loosen up your initial not many yarns, so plan on putting resources into a decent manufactured yarn that is modest. Save those beautiful yarns for when you are more capable. Part of the delight of your later tasks will be rushing to the store to get a showy, fun, astounding chunk of yarn and revel in the delight of working with it, saving the personality of the strands. Test your abilities on modest yarns so you can utilize your imaginative muscles with the expensive ones. Side note: simply don't accepting the very modest, acrylic yarn. This doesn't function admirably for some tasks, particularly beginner ones. All things being equal, settle on a basic regular fiber.

Become a close acquaintence with the Basics

Once more, stay away from the overwhelmed decisions of yarn. These are bad starter yarns. All things being equal, pal up to the essential choices.

Utilize your inventive muscle with an intense shading decision on the off chance that you struggle tolerating the straightforwardness now however attempt to keep the shading light. Interestingly, you consider your to be as you practice, and a lighter yarn shading will make it more evident when you miss a line or commit an error.

Get Curious About New Ideas

The magnificence of sewing today is that there is a plenty of strategies and choices out there for you to explore different avenues regarding. As you are learning, this present time is an incredible opportunity to evaluate some pleasant thoughts. At the point when you are following an example and it tosses a test at you, try it out. Headings for links and yarns over may panic you from the get go, however when you get into them, you will discover they are not unreasonably awful. Additionally, did you begin sewing for simply basic scarves? Presumably not! Thus, this is an ideal opportunity to vanquish your apprehension about an abatement and sew those lovely caps.

Quest for Inspiration and Enjoy the Creativity

Scour Pinterest, tail sewing web journals, peruse pictures of sewed ventures to become roused with what you will sew one day. Ponder extending your collection of sewing undertakings to incorporate headbands, gloves, and other fun "novice" projects. Many destinations will permit you to look through their example information base by expertise level so you can discover projects that you can finish at this stage and comical over projects that you need to challenge yourself with as you continue to rehearse. This assists you with discovering new tasks as well as when dissatisfaction and weariness kick in, you can look through your #1 spots to reignite the fantasy you have of turning into a magnificent knitter.

Utilize Your Resources

In case you are getting baffled with something, look at the pages of this book for tips on the most proficient method to achieve it or put in almost no time on YouTube watching a video to nail that purl. You don't have to experience alone. This and different assets are out there to get you to where you need to be. All else falls flat. Toss it in a sack and bring it into your nearby yarn shop and get some guidance! Possibly join a sewing bunch nearby so you have a local area of knitters to assist you with learning the subtle strategies.

Set It Aside Before Someone (Or Something) Gets Hurt!

You have weaved and eliminated fastens for what feels like hours are as yet not past the principal line of lines. You simply need to toss it and cry. Take a full breath—this has occurred (frequently still does) to us all. Set your weaving to the side, take a bit (or a great deal) an ideal opportunity to yourself, and afterward return at it again when you are prepared. In the event that you attempt to control through the dissatisfaction, you will most likely agreement "insane knitter fit" and will taint your venture with it. You will get so irritated with the one slipped fasten that you will continue to mess up the same way all through the task, and it once in a while closes well. Coming at the issue with quiet and rested eyes will frequently assist you with tackling the issue, essentially simpler than previously, and get you rolling once more.

Know Your Abbreviations or if nothing else Have a Cheat Sheet Handy

As you progress in your sewing profession, you will most likely continue on to designs. A considerable lot of your examples will clarify the truncations they use, however some will not. On the off chance that you don't have a lot of involvement in sewing designs, it might look like nonsense to you. This is a basic fix: keep a rundown of shortenings and a short depiction of what they are. Add new terms and join to the rundown as you go. Reserve this rundown in your weaving supplies so you can add or reference it as you are working.

Clutch Your Practice Projects

As you are learning, you will have a lot of ventures that simply don't turn out feature commendable. That is typical and really something to be thankful for.

However, rather than throwing those training projects, consider dismantling them to reuse the yarn for another task or utilizing portions of them in another art in case there are salvageable pieces. Upcycle or reuse these activities later as you become more gifted. In any event, when you are a knitter either middle or progressed, you will have practice undertakings and cash over the long haul.

Unwind! This Is Supposed to Be Fun

Weaving can be unwinding and fun, or you could allow it to worry you and cause nervousness. You ought to pick weaving for the last mentioned. Anyway, consider the possibility that you mess up. Ignore it! Weaving sets aside time and practice, so the more you gain from it, the better you will get. Partake in the ride. You can lose yourself in reiteration, and you can challenge yourself with novel thoughts. Adventure out and attempt it; you will be astonished at how rapidly you will abandon thinking this is excessively hard to, "Is this actually all it is?!"

Chapter 14: Basic Techniques For Knitting

A few group say there are a few kinds of weaving lines; nonetheless, there is truly just one sew line with varieties to it. This incorporates the purl fasten that you likely have heard a bit about as of now! It truly is only an adaptation of a conventional weave join. Along these lines, breathe a sigh of relief, you just need to dominate one line and afterward have some good times figuring out how to stir it up a tad Stay away from the surprised decisions of yarn. These are bad starter yarns. All things considered, mate up to the fundamental choices.

Utilize your imaginative muscle with an intense shading decision on the off chance that you struggle tolerating the straightforwardness now however attempt to keep the shading light. Interestingly, you consider your to be as you practice, and a lighter yarn shading will make it more clear when you miss a fasten or commit an error. Worsted weight fleece is perhaps the most essential choices you can go with.

Loading Stitch S

kill Level: Beginner

Yarn: Any

Needle: Straight Type

Devices: N/A

The Stockinette Stitch is comprised of weave and purl join. This join has a much smoother appearance than the Garter line however tends to twist, so it's more qualified to moved sleeve and rolled edged scarves.

While making the Stockinette Stitch, recollect that there is a 'right side' and a 'off-base side'. On the 'right side' the fasten will resemble 'angular' shapes.

Stage 1 - Cast on and sew the entirety of the lines in the primary line.

Stage 2 - Swap the needles so the needle with the join is back in your left hand.

Stage 3 - Purl the line of lines.

Stage 4 - Swap the needles again and sew the line.

Stage 5 - Continue to substitute until you have finished the proper number of lines.

Stage 6 - Once you have completed, then, at that point tie off to complete the undertaking.

Strap Stitch

The Garter Stitch Scarf

To begin this task, get a bunch of sewing needles and a ball or two of yarn and cast on. Continue to sew to and fro with supporter lines and tie off when you are finished. Assuming you need to attempt another adaptation, think about switching around the fasten to an essential weave or purl.

Adhere to similar fundamental directions and make a couple less difficult scarves.

Picking a training project like this permits you to evaluate your cast on and tie off abilities, just as wonderful your weaving procedure for a portion of the more essential sews.

The Stocking Knit Washcloth

An additional training project is the staying sew washcloth. This can be a scary task. Relax in the event that it begins to twist as you work, this is typical!

Here is a more itemized example and Instructions:

Supplies:

1 100% cotton yarn, 2.5 ounces skein

7 US sewing needle pair

Scissors

Measure and size:

Measure—20 S (join) and 27 R (columns) per 4 inches. Not basic yet keep as close as could really be expected. More tight washcloths are liked over looser sews, so attempt to keep it near this check.

Size—12 ¼-inch wide x 11-inch long.

Directions:

1. Cast on 61 fastens.

2. Line 1—Knit totally across the front side.

3. Line 2—Use a 1 x 1 rib sew, sew one fasten, and purl the across the whole line.

4. Continue to rehash Steps 2 and 3 until your yarn is practically gone. Tie off.

5. For the overabundance yarn, cut it back and weave in the last details. You are finished!

- Seed st (greenery)

The greenery join – now and again known as a seed fasten – is a simple to make line, which creates superbly complex looking outcomes. Follow headings for how to finish a greenery fasten design underneath.

Cast on a considerably number of join.

Line 1: Alternate between weaving 1 join and purling 1 line across the column.

Line 2: Alternate between purling 1 join and weaving 1 line across the column.

Rehash Rows 1 and 2 for design. When working the greenery or seed fasten, you shift back and forth among weave and purl join in each column. The secret to making the little "seeds" is to sew in the purl join of the column and purl in the weave lines of the line.

Twofold Seed Stitch

Ability Level: Beginner

Yarn: Any

Needle: Straight Type

Apparatuses: N/A

A considerably number of fastens ought to be projected on. In the right-hand side of Row 1, Knit 1 and Purl 1 as far as possible.

Rehash Row # 1 in Row 2.

In Row 3, purl 1 and Knit 1 and rehash as far as possible.

Rehash Row # 3 in Row 4.

Make a reiteration from columns 1 through to the fourth. Rehash from column 1 to 4 till the length you want.

Increment and Decrease

Subsequent to learning the rudiments of weaving and purling, just as the mix of both, you might need to add some zest by making deductions and options to your venture. There are various strategies for expanding and diminishing the lines.

Sew toward the Front and Back

1. Otherwise called "kfb", the sew toward the front and back increment is finished by first making a weave line. Be that as it may, hold the line back from sliding off the left needle.

2. After you make a fasten on the right needle while the other join is as yet on the other left, finish the sew increment by weaving towards the rear of the more established line on the left needle. Similarly, the join being shaped to the back is equivalent to on the facade of the circle. You just did the weaving on the back piece of the circle, behind the needle.

3. When you get two join on the right needle, finish it by sliding the first fasten off the other needle. Presently you have expanded a solitary fasten.

Purl in Front and the Back

Otherwise called "pfb", the purl in front and the back is one method of expanding the lines all the more without any problem. At the point when you do a purl in front and back, you don't do it intuitively as when weaving albeit the method is simply comparative.

In doing a purl toward the front and the back, you likewise start by purling fastens directly through the circle toward the front, having the line at the left needle. While purling through the back, just circle the other needle around so you can work with it through the back circle in a passed on to right bearing. These means will feel very off-kilter from the outset, yet when you become acclimated to it, you'd make more purls as an afterthought in a matter of moments.

Yarn Over

Doing a yarn over is likewise an effective way for expanding lines. This technique creates a hold when sewing and is known as a mix for diminishing in 'sew two together'. This empowers knitters to ensure that the quantity of fastens is comparable across lines.

Then again, in delivering a yarn over between two join, you need to envelop the right needle with the yarn by a back to front way and a counterclockwise bearing prior to beginning each sew fasten. The join that follow are done as would be expected. At the point when you make it to yarning over for the column, do it in a typical join.

At the point when you do a yarn over, it is only equivalent to when you are weaving or purling the accompanying join. At the point when you are sewing, you basically fold the needle over the yarn and have it at the back. Then again, while purling, you need to wrap the needle with the yarn and have the yarn back in the front where it will be purled.

Make One

Otherwise called M1, 'make one' is a famous strategy for expanding sewing join. Make one remaining is condensed as M1L while make one right is curtailed as M1R. This technique is done in the middle of join, and the bar additionally between fastens.

In making a M1L, get the left-hand needle and afterward get the bar from front to the back, in the middle of join. Utilizing your right needle, weave the bar utilizing a back circle. Then again, to make a M1R, simply lift the bar from the back to the front and sew the bar utilizing a front circle.

Utilizing similar lines, you can do this by purling the side. Purl the back circle for a M1L and a front circle for a M1R.

Weave Two Together

A weave two together is the least complex technique for diminishing the join. It diminishes and makes a slight inclination to one side and is generally joined with the SSK or the slip weave technique, which is likewise used to diminish fastens and make an inclination to one side, coming about to try and diminishes on the two sides of the sewed piece. In weaving two together, it resembles making an ordinary sew fasten. The solitary distinction is that you work on two fastens as opposed to doing only one. Weave two together is otherwise called K2Tog.

Purl Two Together

As in sewing two together, you can likewise purl two together and get a similar outcome on the purling side. In making a purl two together, simply embed the right needle on the two circles on the left that follow, as though you were to purl. Do it in the very same manner as you would do in an ordinary purl line. In the wake of completing two fastens, you presently have one. The purl two together is otherwise called P2Tog.

Slip Knit

The slip sew is likewise a one of the least difficult and most essential way for diminishing lines. It makes a diminishing and an inclination to one side. It is generally utilized alongside weave two together which makes an inclination abatement to one side.

In doing a slip weave, simply slip the absolute first line like you planned to sew, then, at that point slip again the second join as you were to sew. Then, at that point have the needle on the passed on slide to the front of the two fastens and do a weave join of both. Slip sew has a condensing of SSK.

Pushing Off

Pushing off is likewise a significant ability to master, and this is done when you've finished either the task or that you're chipping away at and need to get it totally off your needles. Restricting off is another word for pushing off, and you'll see the two terms utilized in various examples. Simply recollect not to do it too firmly assuming you need to proceed. Start by sewing the initial two join, and afterward embed the mark of your left needle into the principal line, pulling it throughout the second. The subsequent fasten will then, at that point be off of your needle. This cycle ought to be proceeded until you're toward the finish of the line, and afterward you can get the yarn through the last fasten, expecting you to pull it up, and leave a tail that is around six inches long. This will be worked into your venture.

Conclusion

The workmanship known as macrame is the specialty of tying an assortment of mathematical plans without utilizing snares, needles, or loops.

The macrame ability traces all the way back to the thirteenth century. The word macrame is initially Arabic, which signifies "periphery." It is accepted that the capacity was started by Arabian weavers by tying the extra substance at the edges of loamed fiber. From such sources in the mid fourteenth and fifteenth hundreds of years, it at last came to Italy and France. Mariners got the capacity since it was a most loved approach to pass a portion of the extended periods of time adrift. The straightforward bunches utilized by the mariners today are a similar macrame ties ... the half bunch, square bunch, and the half snare hitch. The mariners passed on their techniques to the Chinese, who fit the mastery with their own exceptional traditions and culture. During the nineteenth century, ability was well known with the British.

The capacities dropped to disappointment with the progression of time. It was reestablished during the 1960s and 1970s, carrying rejuvenation to the antiquated abilities. Its prominence dropped some during the 80s and 90s, however the start of the 21st century saw its ubiquity return to going full speed ahead, with a limitless number of imaginative opportunities for the specialist, craftsman, and appreciator of the various assorted macrame items.

Nowadays the workmanship and capacity of macrame mean different things to various people. There are an assortment of reasons the ability is helpful for other people. Tying the different bunches can reinforce hands and arms. Making a macrame undertaking will deliver the brain, body, and soul extremely loose! Macrame adventures call for not many assets and guarantee materials with no added substances or exhaust; it is an earth-accommodating, regular ability undoubtedly.

Macrame plans contrast with caps, holders for trees, home furnishings, holders for entryways, handbags, and belts. Macrame tones and surfaces outfit a wide assortment of decisions. Materials range from differing jute and hemp thicknesses to twine, shaded nylon, and polyester filaments. There are wooden globules in projects these days as well as glass and earthenware dots are fused into projects also.

Macrame has changed, indeed, it's all essential for the innovative, staggered measure that perseveres. Just as specialists, amateur macrame skilled workers think that it is remedial, fun, inventive, and fulfilling. There are an ever increasing number of decisions for better macrame than expand the stylistic theme of your home, closet, and individual style for the individuals who simply need to utilize and like the finished pieces.

Printed in Great Britain
by Amazon